British Museum

A Guide to the Autograph Letters, Manuscripts, Original Charters

And Royal, Baronial, and Ecclesiastical Seals Exhibited in the Department of Manuscripts and in the King's Library

British Museum

A Guide to the Autograph Letters, Manuscripts, Original Charters
And Royal, Baronial, and Ecclesiastical Seals Exhibited in the Department of Manuscripts and in the King's Library

ISBN/EAN: 9783337104986

Printed in Europe, USA, Canada, Australia, Japan

Cover: Foto ©Andreas Hilbeck / pixelio.de

More available books at **www.hansebooks.com**

BRITISH MUSEUM.

A GUIDE

TO THE

AUTOGRAPH LETTERS,

MANUSCRIPTS, ORIGINAL CHARTERS,

AND

ROYAL, BARONIAL, AND ECCLESIASTICAL SEALS

EXHIBITED IN THE

DEPARTMENT OF MANUSCRIPTS

AND IN

THE KING'S LIBRARY.

PRINTED BY ORDER OF THE TRUSTEES.

1887.

LONDON:
PRINTED BY WILLIAM CLOWES AND SONS, LIMITED,
STAMFORD STREET AND CHARING CROSS.

CONTENTS.

AUTOGRAPHS:—

PAGE

I.—English and Foreign Eminent Men 5

II.—English Sovereigns 11

III.—British Statesmen and Commanders 18

IV.—Historical 24

V.—Literary 29

VI.—Literary Works, etc. 35

ORIGINAL CHARTERS 39

MANUSCRIPTS:—

I.—Greek 43

II.—Latin, etc. 46

III.—English 53

IV.—Oriental 55

EARLY BIBLICAL MSS. 60

HISTORICAL DEEDS AND PAPYRI 61

MISCELLANEOUS DOCUMENTS 63

SEALS 64

ILLUMINATIONS 73

DEPARTMENT OF MANUSCRIPTS.

AUTOGRAPHS.*

[Commencing with the cases on the left hand, as the visitor enters from the Grenville Library.]

I.—ENGLISH AND FOREIGN EMINENT MEN.

1. DESIDERIUS ERASMUS. [b. 1467—d. 1536.] Letter, in *Latin*, to Nicholas Everard, President of Holland, on Luther's marriage, etc. "Solent Comici tumultus fere in matrimonium exire, atque hinc subita rerum omnium tranquillitas . . . Similem exitum habitura videtur Lutherana Tragœdia. Duxit uxorem, monachus monacham . . . Luterus nunc mitior esse incipit, nec perinde sevit calamo." Dated, Basel, 24 Dec. 1525. *Holograph;* with the signature "ERASMUS Rot[erodamus] vere tuus, ex tempore manu propria." [*Egerton MS.* 1863, f. 2.]
2. MARTIN LUTHER. [b. 1481—d. 1546.] Letter, in *Latin*, to Thomas Cromwell, Secretary of State, excusing himself for not replying to a letter sent by Dr. Barnes, on account of the sudden departure of the latter, and rejoicing in Cromwell's zeal for the cause of Christ and his power to advance it. Dated, Wittenberg, Palm Sunday, 1536. *Holograph.* [*Harley MS.* 6989, f. 35.]
3. PHILIP MELANCTHON. [b. 1497—d. 1560.] Letter, in *Latin*, to Henry VIII, sending him a book by the hands of Alexander Alesius, the Scotchman, and expressing admiration of his talent and virtue. Dated Aug. 1535. *Holograph;* with the signature: "Regiæ Maiestati tuæ addictissimus PHILIPPUS MELANTHON." [*Harley MS.* 6989, f. 54.]

* N.B. When a letter or document is entirely in one hand it is marked as *Holograph*.

4. John Calvin. [b. 1509—d. 1564.] Letter, in *Latin*, to Guillaume Farel, pastor of the church of Neufchatel, in recommendation of the bearer as a school teacher. Dated, Geneva, 8 Dec. 1551. *Holograph.* [*Add. MS.* 12,100, f. 6.]
5. Sir Thomas More. [b. 1480—d. 1535.] Letter to Henry viii., reminding him that "at such tyme as of that great weighty rome and office of your chauncellour . . . ye were so good and graciouse unto me as, at my pore humble suit, to discharge and disburden me, geving me licence with your graciouse favour to bestow the residew of my life, in myn age now to come, abowt the provision for my soule," the king had promised him his favour; and now praying "that of your accustumed goodnes no sinistre information move your noble grace to have eny more distruste of my trouth and devotion toward you than I have or shall duryng my life geve the cause"; that in the matter of "the wykked woman of Canterbury" [Elizabeth Barton, the Maid of Kent] he had declared the truth to Cromwell; that if the King believes him guilty he is ready to forfeit life and fortune, his compensation being that after his short life and the King's long life, "I shold onys mete with your grace agayn in hevyn and there be mery with you"; but that, if the King thinks that he has acted according to duty, he will relieve him from the Bill brought against him in Parliament. Dated, "at my pore howse in Chelchith," 5 March [1534]. *Holograph.* [*Cotton MS.* Cleopatra E. vi. f. 176.]
6. Thomas Cranmer, Archbishop of Canterbury. [b. 1489—d. 1556.] Letter to [Thomas, Lord Cromwell], thanking him "that your Lordeship at my requeste hath not only exhibited the [English] Bible which I sent unto you to the Kinges maiestie, but also hath obteigned of his grace that the same shalbe alowed by his auctoritie to be bowghte and redde within this realme . . . assuryng your Lordeship for the contentacion of my mynde you have shewid me more pleasour herin than yf you hadd given me a thowsande pownde." Dated, Ford, 13 Aug. [1537]. *Signed* "Your own bowndman ever T. Cantuarien." [*Cotton MS.* Cleop. E. v. f. 348.]
7. Sir Francis Drake [b. 1540—d. 1596] and Sir John Hawkins [b. 1520—d. 1595]. Certificate that Sir

Thomas Baskerville is an adventurer to the amount of £500 "in this vioadge to be (by Godes permission) perfourmed into forrayne partes with sixe of her Ma[tes] shippes and soundrie other marchantes shipps latelie commytted to our chardge." Dated, 24 July, 37 Elizabeth [1595]. *Signed*, and with seals. [*Harley MS.* 4762, f. 132.]

8. Sir Walter Raleigh. [b. 1552—d. 1618.] Letter to Lord Burghley on the value of prizes captured by ships of Sir John Watts and others, and on the partition of profits which are very small: "This is the very trewth, I asure your L[ordship] before the livinge God, as nire as wee can sett down or gett knowledge of. Of which, if ought should be taken, ther would never our men of warr put out; and so all our shipps may rote, our mariners run awaye, and her Maiesty lose the best part of her custome." "From Derum House, this xvi. of October [1591]." *Holograph.* [*Lansdowne MS.* 69, f. 60.]

9. Michelangelo Buonarroti. [b. 1474—d. 1564.] Letter, in *Italian*, to Lodovico di Buonarrota Simoni, his father, contradicting a rumour of his death, complaining that he has received no money from the Pope for 13 months, and referring to an action at law of Monna Cassandra, his aunt; [June, A.D. 1508]. *Holograph;* with signature, "Vostro Michelagniolo in Roma." [*Add. MS.* 23,140, f. 6.]

10. Albert Dürer. [b. 1471—d. 1528.] Letter to Wilbolt Pirkamer [Bilibald Pirckheimer], of Nuremberg, relative to a painting of the Virgin Mary; [written from Venice, and] dated on the Wednesday after St Matthew's day [23rd Sept.], 1506. *Holograph.* [*Harl. MS.* 4935, f. 41.]

11. Peter Paul Rubens. [b. 1577—d. 1640.] Letter, in *Italian*, to [— Dupuy?] on the defeat of the English at La Rochelle, thanking him for letters of J. L. Guez, Sieur de Balzac, criticising the latter's "Censor," etc. Dated, Antwerp, 30 Dec. 1627. *Holograph;* with the signature, "Pietro Pauolo Rubens." [*Add. MS.* 18,741, f. 101.]

12. Anthony Van Dyck. [b. 1599—d. 1641.] Letter, in *Dutch*, to Francis Junius, the younger, in praise of his work "De Pictura Veterum," and requesting him to

supply a Latin motto for an engraved portrait of Sir Kenelm Digby. Dated 14 Aug. 1636. *Holograph.* [*Harley MS.* 4935, f. 45.]

13. PAUL REMBRANDT VAN RYN. [b. 1608—d. 1669.] Letter, in *Dutch*, to [Constantine Huygens] Heer van Zuylichem, Secretary to the Prince of Orange, asking for payment of a sum due to him; *n. d.* *Holograph.* [*Add. MS.* 23,744, f. 3.]

14. SIR PHILIP SIDNEY. [b. 1554—d. 1588.] Letter to [Lord Burghley?] on the condition of his garrison of Flushing: "The garrison is weak; the people by thes cross fortunes crossly disposed; and this is y[e] conclusion: if these 2 places be kept, her Ma[ti] hath worth her monei in all extremities; if thei shoold be lost, none of the rest wold hold a dai." Dated, Flushing, 14 Aug. 1586. *Holograph.* [*Stowe MS.* 355.]

15. SIR FRANCIS BACON. [b. 1561—d. 1626.] Letter to Sir Michael Hicks, informing him that a commission on the King's service would sit at his house: "It will take up a whole afternoon, and thearfore no remedy, but we must dyne with you"; [6 Aug. 1609]. *Holograph.* [*Lansdowne MS.* 91, f. 93].

16. GALILEO GALILEI. [b. 1564—d. 1642.] Letter, in *Italian*, to Michelangelo Buonarroti, thanking him for his letter, hoping to be with him before St. John's day, and referring to his improvement in the construction of spectacles. Dated, Padua, 4 Dec. 1609. *Holograph.* [*Add. MS.* 23,139, f. 39.]

17. SIR ISAAC NEWTON. [b. 1642—d. 1727.] Letter to William Briggs, M.D., commending his "New Theory of Vision," but dissenting from certain positions in it: "I have perused your very ingenious Theory of Vision, in which (to be free with you as a friend should be) there seems to be some things more solid and satisfactory, others more disputable, but yet plausibly suggested and well deserving the consideration of the ingenious," etc. Dated, Trinity College, Cambridge, 20 June, 1682. *Holograph.* [*Add. MS.* 4237, f. 32.]

18. PRINCE RUPERT. [b. 1619—d. 1682.] Letter to Sir Edward Nicholas, Secretary of State, referring to reflections upon him as being unfavourable to open counsels; and on military movements. Dated, Bristol, 5 July [1645]. *Holograph;* partly in cipher, with de-

cipherings by Sir E. Nicholas. [*Add. MS.* 18,738, f. 80.]

19. SIR EDWARD HYDE, afterward EARL OF CLARENDON. [b. 1608—d. 1674.] Letter to the Earl of Winchilsea, assuring him that "I had never any apprehension that I should continue longe in your displeasure upon the misrepresentacion I hearde had bene very maliciously made to your lordshipp concerninge me," etc. Dated, Breda, 23 May [1660]. *Holograph.* [*Add. MS.* 32,093, f. 421.]

20. JEAN BAPTISTE POQUELIN MOLIÈRE. [b. 1622—d. 1673.] Notarial Certificate, in *French*, signed by him and Jacques Martin, relative to the disposition of the goods of Françoise Rousseau, deceased. Dated 25 Jan. 1664. [*Add. MS.* 24,419, f. 2.]

21. JOHN DRYDEN. [b. 1631—d. 1700.] Letter to [Laurence Hyde, Earl of Rochester, First Lord of the Treasury]: "I know not whether my Lord Sunderland has interceded with your Lordship for half a yeare of my salary. But I have two other advocates, my extreame wants, even almost to arresting, and my ill health. . . . . If I durst I wou'd plead a little merit and some hazards of my life . . . . but I onely thinke I merite not to sterve. . . . . Be pleasd to looke on me with an eye of compassion; some small employment wou'd render my condition easy. The king is not unsatisfyed of me, the Duke has often promised me his assistance; and your Lordship is the conduit through which their favours passe. Either in the Customes or the Appeales of the Excise, or some other way; meanes cannot be wanting, if you please to have the will. 'Tis enough for one age to have neglected Mr Cowley and sterv'd Mr Buttler." [A.D. 1683?] *Holograph.* [*Add. MS.* 17,017, f. 49.]

22. JONATHAN SWIFT, DEAN OF ST. PATRICK'S. [b. 1667—d. 1745.] Playful letter to Martha Blount. . . . "I long to see you a London Lady where you are forcd to wear whole cloaths and visit in a chair, for which you must starve next summer at Petersham with a mantau out at the sides, and spunge once a week at our house without ever inviting us in a whole season to a cow-heel at home. I wish you would bring Mr Pope over with you when you come, but we will leave Mr Gay to his beggars and his operaes till he is able to pay his club." . . . Dated,

Dublin, 29 Feb. 1727–8. *Holograph ;* without signature. [*Stowe MS.* 676.]

23. JOSEPH ADDISON. [b. 1672—d. 1719.] Letter, as Secretary of State, to George Bubb, Envoy to Spain, desiring him, if he had any further conversation with "Monsr d'Alberoni on the subject of an Accommodation between the Emperor and King of Spain by the interposition of his Majesty, to send me an account of it in a separate letter without mixing it with any other matters." Dated, Cockpitt, 22 Apr. 1717. *Holograph.* [*Egerton MS.* 2174, f. 166.]

24. Sir RICHARD STEELE. [b. 1671—d. 1729.] Letter to Henry Pelham, asking whether the Duke of Newcastle will recall the order of silence imposed upon Drury Lane Theatre; "but if My Lord insists to keep me out of my right, I must plainly tell you, that is, His Grace by you, that the right of petitioning the King in Council, the Parliament sitting, or the Judges in Westminster Hall, shall be utterly taken from me before I will suffer my very good Lord to send my children a starving." Dated 27 May, 1720. *Holograph.* [*Newcastle Papers.*] *Presented, in* 1886, *by the Earl of Chichester.*

25. ALEXANDER POPE. [b. 1688—d. 1744.] Letter to Rev. [William] Warburton, referring to Lord Bolingbroke's departure: "He went for Calais 4 days since, with a strong purpose never to return. The Learned World will gain by what the Political World has lost." Dated 18 June [1735.] *Holograph.* [*Egerton MS.* 1946, f. 48.]

26. FRANÇOIS MARIE AROUET DE VOLTAIRE. [b. 1694—d. 1778.] Letter, in *English*, to George Keate, F.R.S., expressing friendship and passing remarks on the literary position of England and France: "Had I not fix'd the seat of my retreat in the free corner of Geneva, I would certainly live in the free kingdom of England, for, tho I do not like the monstruous irregularities of Shakespear, tho I admire but some lively and masterly strokes in his performances, yet I am confident no body in the world looks with a greater veneration on y^r good philosophers, on the croud of y^r good authors, and I am these thirty years the disciple of y^r way of thinking. Y^r nation is at once a people of warriours and of philosophers. You are now at the pitch of glory in regard to publick affairs. But I know not wether you have pre-

serv'd the reputation y[r] island enjoy'd in point of litterature when Adisson, Congreve, Pope, Swift, were alive." Dated, Aux Délices, 16 Jan. 1760. *Holograph.* [*Add. MS.* 30,991, f. 13.] *Bequeathed, in* 1879, *by John Henderson, Esq.*

27. George Washington. [b. 1732—d. 1799.] Letter, as Colonel in the English service commanding the troops of Virginia, to Brigadier-General H. Bouquet, relative to military movements against the French: "I coud wish most sincerely that our rout was fixd that we might be in motion, for we are all of us most heartily tird and sick of inactivity." Dated, Camp at Fort Cumberland, 28 Aug. 1758. *Holograph.* [*Add. MS.* 21,641, f. 52.] *Presented, in* 1857, *by William Haldimand, Esq.*

28. Napoléon I., Emperor of the French. Letter to Marshal [André] Massena [afterwards Duc de Rivoli and Prince d'Esslingen] on his movements against Ostrolenka [in Russian Poland], and directing him to attack the enemy. Dated, Finckenstein, 17 May, 1807. Signed "Napoleon"; with the following *holograph* postscript: "6000 hommes qui avoient voulu penetrer par la langue de terre de Pillau a Danzig ont été defait hier 16; nous leur avons pris 900 hommes et 4 pièces de canon." [*Add. MS.* 22,723, f. 17.]

II.—ENGLISH SOVEREIGNS.

29. Richard II. Particulars of agreement, in *French*, for the restoration of the castle of Brest to the Duke of Brittany [A.D. 1397]. Signed by the King "le Roy R. S." *i.e.* "Richard Second." [*Cotton MS.* Vesp. F. iii. f. 3.]

30. Henry IV. Letter, in *French*, to his Council in London, announcing that "la Dame Spenser [Constance, widow of Thomas Despencer, Earl of Gloucester] et lez enfauntz de la Marche [Edmund Mortimer, Earl of March, and Roger his brother, confined at Windsor] sount fuyez par Abyndon" on their way to Glamorgan and Cardiff, and ordering the arrest of a squire named Morgan whom they had sent to Flanders and France,

if he should still be in London. Dated "a nostre chastiell de Wynd[sor] en hast yceste dismenge matyn" [? 14 Feb. 1406]. Signed by the king "H. R., nous prions penser de la mer." [*Cotton MS.* Vesp. F. iii. f. 4.]

31. HENRY V. Portion of a letter, as follows:—"Furthremore I wold that ye comend with my brothre, with the chanceller, with my cosin of Northumbrelond, and my cosin of Westmerland; and that ye set a gode ordinance for my north marches, and specialy for the Duc of Orlians and for alle the remanant of my prisoners of France, and also for the K[ing] of Scotelond, for, as I am secrely enfourmed by a man of ryght notable estate in this lond that there hath ben a man of the Duces of Orliance in Scotland and accorded with the Duc of Albany, that this next somer he schal bryng in the maumet of Scotlond to sturre what he may, and also that ther schold be founden weys to the havyng awey specialy of the Duc of Orlians, and also of ther K[ing], as welle as of the remanant of my forsayd prysoners; that God do defende. Wherfore I wolle that the Duc of Orliance be kept stille within the castil of Pontfret with owte goyng to Robertis place or to any othre disport, for it is bettre he lak his disport then we were disceyved. Of alle the remanant dothe as ye thenketh." [A.D. 1419?] *Holograph.* [*Cotton MS.* Vesp. F. iii. f. 5.]

32. HENRY VI. Inspeximus, in *Latin*, confirming a grant by Queen Joanna [of Navarre, widow of Henry IV.] to Edmund Beaufort, Earl of Mortaigne, for the term of her life, of the offices of Constable of Nottingham Castle and Keeper of Sherwood Forest, 20 Jan., 3 Hen. VI. [1425], and an assignment of the same by the said Earl to Ralph, Lord Cromwell, 12 June, 12 Hen. VI. [1434], and prolonging the latter's term after the death of the Queen, if he should survive her. Dated, Westminster, 14 Feb., a° 15 [1437]. Signed at the top by the King "R. H. nous avons grante." [*Cotton MS.* Vesp. F. xiii. f. 41.]

33. EDWARD IV. Memorandum touching the repayment of one hundred marks to the Bishop of Aberdeen and to James Shaw, for the composition made with [Sir John Colquhoun] Lord of Luss, that "the king hath ordeigned that a Lumbard or somme othre sufficient persone or

persones resiant within England shalbe bounde . . . in the saide somme to be paied by the first daye of Novembre next to come at the ferrest." [A.D. 1472?] Signed at the head and at the foot by the King "R. E." [*Cotton MS.* Vesp. F. iii. f. 9 b.]

34. EDWARD V. A slip of vellum [cut from a volume] containing the three inscriptions, "R. Edwardus quintus"; "Loyaulte me lie. Richard Gloucestre" [Richard, Duke of Gloucester, afterwards RICHARD III.]; and "Souente me souenne. Harre Bokyngham" [Henry Stafford, Duke of Buckingham]; [Apr.—June, 1483]. [*Cotton MS.* Vesp. F. xiii. f. 53.]

35. HENRY VII. Letter, in *Latin*, to King Ferdinand and Queen Isabella of Spain, acknowledging the receipt of their letters in which they announce their agreement to the contract of marriage of the Princess Katherine with Arthur, Prince of Wales, and their intention of sending her to England at the end of the summer, etc. Dated, Canterbury, 20 June, 1500. Signed by the King "HENRICUS R." [*Egerton MS.* 616, f. 19.]

36. HENRY VIII. Letter to "myne awne good Cardinall" Wolsey, as follows: "I recomande me unto yow with all my hart and thanke yow for the grette payne and labour that yow do dayly take in my bysynes and maters, desyryng yow (that wen yow have well establyssyd them) to take summe pastyme and comfort, to the intente yow may the lenger endure to serve us, for allways payne cannott be induryd. Surly yow have so substancyally orderyd oure maters bothe off thys syde the see and byonde that in myne oppynion lityll or no thyng can be addyd...Wryttyn with the hand off your lovyng master HENRY R." [March, 1518.] [*Cotton MS.* Vesp. F. xiii. f. 71.]

37. KATHERINE OF ARAGON, QUEEN OF HENRY VIII. Letter to her daughter, the Princess Mary, on the state of her health, etc.: "As for your writing in Lattine, I am glad that ye shall chaunge frome me to Maister Federston, for that shall doo you moche good, to lerne by hym to write right; but yet some tymes I wold be glad, when ye doo write to Maister Federston of your owne enditings, when he hathe rede it, that I may se it, for it shalbe a grete comfort to me to see you kepe your Latten and fayer writing and all." Dated "at Obourne [Wo-

burn?] this Fryday night." [1525?] In a secretary's hand; signed by the Queen "Your loving mother KATHERINA THE QWENE." [*Cotton MS.* Vesp. F. xiii. f. 72.]

38. ANNE BOLEYN, QUEEN OF HENRY VIII. Letter, written before her marriage with the King, to Cardinal Wolsey, thanking him "for the gret payn and travell that your grace doth take in stewdyeng by your wysdome and gret dylygens howe to bryng to pas honerably the gretyst welth that is possyble to come to any creatour lyvyng, and in especyall remembryng howe wrecchyd and unworthy I am in comparyng to his hyghnes," and promising "that after this matter is brought to pas you shall fynd me, as I am bownd in the meane tym, to owe you my servyse, and then looke what thyng in this woreld I can inmagen to do you pleasor in, you shall fynd me the gladdyst woman in the woreld to do yt." [A.D. 1528—1530.] *Holograph.* [*Cotton MS.* Vesp. F. xiii. f. 73.]

39. EDWARD VI. "Lycence and pasport" for "Mr Doctour Burgarte, Mr Doctour Bruno, and Mr James Lersner, who repayred hither in ambassade [from the Protestant States of Germany] in the tyme of our derest Father," to "returne into the parties of beyonde the sees" with "the nombre of xvi^ten^ servauntes and vi horses or geldinges ambling or trotting, their money, plate, juelles, and all other their bagges, baggages and necessaries." Dated "at our pallaice of Westminster", 8 Mar., a° 1 [1547]. In a secretary's hand; signed at the top "EDWARD." Also signed by E[dward Seymour, Duke of] Somerset [Protector], John [Dudley, Earl of] Warwick [afterwards Duke of Northumberland], T[homas Seymour, Lord] Seymour [of Sudely], W[illiam Paulet, Lord] Saint John, J[ohn Russell, Lord] Russell, Cuth[bert Tunstall, Bishop of] Durham, Sir Antony Browne, Sir William Paget, Sir Antony Denny, and Sir W[illiam] Herbert. [*Cotton MS.* Vesp. F. iii. f. 19.]

40. LADY JANE GREY, AS QUEEN. Order to Sir John Bridges and Sir Nicholas Poyntz, to levy forces "and with the same to repaire with all possible spead towardes Buckinghamshire, for the repression and subdewing of certain tumultes and rebellions moved there against us and our Crowne by certain seditious men." Dated,

Tower of London, 18 July, "in the first yere of our reign" [1553]. Signed at the top "JANE THE QUENE." [*Harley MS.* 416, f. 30.]

41. MARY. "Instructions for my lorde previsel [Lord Russell, Lord Privy Seal, sent to receive her husband Philip of Spain, on his landing at Southampton in July 1554]. Fyrste to telle the Kyng the whole state of this Realme with all thynges appartaynyng to the same as myche as ye knowe to be trewe. Seconde to obey his commaundment in all thynges. Thyrdly in all thynges he shall aske your aduyse to decl[are] your opinion as becommeth a faythfull conceyllour to do. MARYE THE QUENE." *Holograph.* [*Cotton MS.* Vesp. F. iii. No. 21.]

42. ELIZABETH. Letter in *French*, to the King of France, referring to the small results of the negotiations of his ambassadors at her Court, and her willingness to favour his views in spite of his disregard of her requests, and adding "vous voyes par la que la necessitie qui vous presse s'advance beaucoup au devant de mes propres affaires, faysant paroistre que suis meilléur Soeur que Royne, et que je oublie que la Charite doit commencer par soy." [A.D. 1576?] *Holograph.* [*Add. MS.* 21,505, f. 17.]

43. JAMES I. Letter to his son, Charles, Prince of Wales, ordering his return home from the Court of Spain, as follows:—"My dearest sonne, I sent you a comandement long agoe not to loose tyme quhaire ye are; but ather to bring quikelie hoame youre mistresse, quhiche is my earnist desyre; but if no bettir maye be, rather then to linger any longer thaire, to come without her, quhiche for manie important reasons I ame now forcid to renew. And thairfor I charge you upon my blessing to come quikelie ather with her or without her. I knowe youre love to her person hath enforcid you to delaye the putting in execution of my former comandement. I confesse it is my cheifest wordlie ioye that ye love her, but the necessitie of my effaires enforcith me to tell you that ye muste præferre the obedience to a father to the love ye carrie to a mistresse. And so God blesse you. JAMES R. Cranburne the 10 of Auguste," [1623]. *Holograph.* [*Harley MS.* 6987, f. 143.]

44. Charles I. Letter to Prince Rupert, thanking him for his letter and the freedom of his remarks, and concluding, "Lastly I shall offer you a fancy of my owen; It is lykely that your Brother Maurice army shall joyne with this; now to avoid disputes, I desyre to know if you thinke it not fitt that I should declare your Brother, in your absence, Generall of my Horse." Dated, Oxford, 26 May, 1644. *Holograph.* [*Add. MS.* 18,983, f. 7.]

45. Oliver Cromwell. Letter to Lord Fairfax, congratulating him on "the prosperitye of your affaires wherin the good of all honest men is soe much concerned," and announcing the capture of Wexford: "The Lord shewes us great mercye heere, indeed Hee, Hee only gave this stronge towne of Wexford into our handes." Dated, Wexford, 15 Oct. 1649. *Holograph.* [*Egerton MS.* 2620, f. 7.]

46. Charles II. Letter to Sir George Downing, English Ambassador at the Hague, giving instructions for his conduct: "I have thought fitt to send you my last minde upon the hinge of your whole negotiation and in my owne hand, that you may likewise know it is your part to obey punctually my orders, instead of putting yourselfe to the trouble of finding reasons why you do not do so. .... But upon the whole matter you must allwaies know my minde and resolution is, not only to insist upon the haveing my flag saluted even on there very shoare (as it was alwaies practised) but in haveing my dominion of the seas asserted, and Van Guent exemplarily punished." Dated, Whitehall, 16 Jan. 167½. *Holograph.* [*Stowe MS.* 458.]

47. James II. Letter to William Henry, Prince of Orange, referring to complicity of certain of the magistrates of Amsterdam in the Duke of Monmouth's rebellion, whose names he would transmit: "When I can gett any authentike proffs against them, I shall lett you have it, wch I feare will be hard to be gott, tho tis certaine some of them knew of the D[uke] of Mon[mouth's] designe." Dated, Windsor, 25 August, 1685. *Holograph.* [*Add. MS.* 28,103, f. 68.]

48. William III. Letter, in *French*, to the Prince de Vaudemont, touching on the prospects of the campaign and the progress of the siege of Namur: "L'onav

ouvrir la trenchée cette nuit du coste de St Nicola," etc. Dated "Au Camp devant Namur ce 11e de Juilliet, 1695, au soir a 9 eures." *Holograph.* [*Add. MS.* 21,493, f. 5.]

49. Mary II. Order, in the absence of William III., to Admiral Arthur [Herbert], Earl of Torrington, to engage the French fleet: "We apprehend y[e] consequences of your retiring to y[e] Gunfleet to be so fatall, y[t] we choose rather y[t] you should upon any advantage of y[e] Wind give battle to y[e] Enemy then retreat farther then is necessary to gett an advantage upon y[e] Enemy." Dated, Whitehall, 29 June, 1690. Signed at the top "Marie R."; and countersigned by [Daniel Finch] Earl of Nottingham, Secretary of State. [*Egerton MS.* 2621, f. 91.]

50. Anne. Letter to [Sidney Godolphin,] Earl of Godolphin, Lord High Treasurer, upon "y[e] Scotch affairs," complaining that "those people use me very hardly in opposseing Lord Forfars being of y[e] Treasury," etc. Dated, Windsor, 14 June [1705]. *Holograph.* [*Add. MS.* 28,070, f. 10.]

51. George I. Letter, in *French*, to the Emperor Charles VI. on the occasion of sending Abraham Stanian as Ambassador to Constantinople. Dated, Hampton Court, 17 October, 1717. *Holograph.* [*Add. MS.* 22,046, f. 48.]

52. George II. Letter to [Thomas Pelham-Holles] 1st Duke of Newcastle, First Lord of the Treasury, referring to the despatch of a messenger [to Germany] and directing the sum of £10,000 to be sent to him. [5 Dec. 1759]. *Holograph.* [*Newcastle Papers.*] *Presented, in* 1886, *by the Earl of Chichester.*

53. George III. Paragraph written out by himself for insertion in his first Speech from the Throne:—"Born and educated in this country, I glory in the name of Britain, and the peculiar happiness of my life will ever consist in promoting the welfare of a people whose loyalty and warm affection to me I consider as the greatest and most permanent security of my Throne." [15 Nov. 1760]. [*Newcastle Papers.*] *Presented, in* 1886, *by the Earl of Chichester.*

54. George IV. Letter to Louis XVIII., King of France, announcing the death of king George III. and his own accession to the throne. Dated, Carlton House, 31 Jan. 1820. Signed by the King, and countersigned by

[Robert] Viscount Castlereagh, Secretary of State. [*Add. MS.* 24,023, f. 60.]

55. William IV. Codicil to the King's will, bequeathing to the Crown all his additions to the libraries in the several royal palaces; 10 July, 1833. With an *autograph* confirmation, signed and sealed by the King, declaring "that all the Books, Drawings, and Plans collected in all the Palaces shall for ever continue Heir-looms to the Crown, and on no pretence whatever to be alienated from the Crown"; dated, Brighton, 30 Nov. 1834. [*Add. MS.* 30,170, f. 8.]

56. Victoria. Autograph Signature of Her Majesty, written in pencil, when Princess Victoria, at the age of four years. [A.D. 1823.] [*Add. MS.* 18,204, f. 12.]

57. Victoria. Summons to Dr. Samuel [Butler], Bishop of Lichfield, to attend Her Majesty's Coronation. Dated, St. James's, 9 May, 1838. Signed by the Queen; and countersigned by [Bernard Edward Howard] Duke of Norfolk, Earl Marshal. [*Add. MS.* 12,093, f. 26.]

III.—BRITISH STATESMEN AND COMMANDERS.

[In the cases at right-angles to those already described.]

58. Cardinal Wolsey. [b. 1471—d. 1530.] Letter written after his disgrace to Stephen [Gardiner, afterwards Bishop of Winchester], making arrangements respecting appointments in the province of York, and continuing "that sythyns in thys and all other thynges I have and do moste obedyently submyt and conforme my sylf to hys graces pleasure" he trusts "yt wole now please his maieste to shewe hys pety, compassyon, and bowntuose goodnes towardes me without sufferyng me any leynger to lye langwyshyng and consumyng awey throwth thys myn extreme sorowe and hevynes." "Wryttyne at Asher [Esher] thys twysday with the rude hand of your dayly bedysman, T[homas] Cardinalis Ebor." [9 March, 1530.] *Holograph.* [*Add. MS.* 25,114, f. 28.]

59. WILLIAM CECIL, LORD BURGHLEY. [b. 1520—d. 1598.] Letter to Sir Christopher Hatton concerning the trial of Mary, Queen of Scots, delivering Queen Elizabeth's pleasure "that ther be no enlargment of hir cryme, butt breffly declared for mayntenance of the endyttment that she allowed of Babyngtons wrytyng or lettre; nether wold she that ether by my L. Cobham, your self, or by any other, any sharp speches be used in condemnation or reprooff of the Scottes Quene cryme." Dated 12 Sept. [1586]. *Holograph.* [*Egerton MS.* 2124, f. 30.]

60. THOMAS WENTWORTH, VISCOUNT WENTWORTH, AFTERWARDS EARL OF STRAFFORD. [b. 1593—d. 1641.] Letter to the Earl of Carlisle: "Ther is upon the way towards your Lordship a whole kennell of houndes; five cople of them are for me, nor was I ever maister of soe many before in all my life. I wishe they prove for your liking; thus much in ther byhalfe according to the dialectt of a Northeren Cracker. Ther ancestors weare of thos famouse Heroes that in the feildes of Hauworth and Wettwange weare of the cheefe in sentte and vewe; and, if it came to a blacke hare, run doggs, horse, and men cleare out of sighte, and the silly beaste was sure to die for it, before shee gott to the tow miles end," etc. Dated, York, 20 Dec. 1632. *Holograph.* [*Egerton MS.* 2597, f. 108.]

61. JOHN HAMPDEN. [b. 1594—d. 1643.] Letter to Colonel Bulstrode and others commanding parliamentary troops: "The army is now at North Hampton, moving every day nearer to you. If you disband not, wee may be a mutuall succour, each to other; but, if you disperse, you make yourselves and your country a pray." Dated, Northampton, 31 Oct. [1642]. [*Stowe MS.* 301.]

62. JOHN CHURCHILL, DUKE OF MARLBOROUGH. [b. 1650—d. 1722.] Letter, in *French*, to George Louis, Elector of Hanover [afterwards George I. of England], giving an account of his victory at Ramillies: "Le combat se shauffa et dura assez long tems avec une tres grand fureur mais enfin les ennemis furent obliges de plier. . . . Ainsi le bon Dieu nous a donné un victoire complet." Dated, Louvain, 25 May, 1706. *Holograph.* [*Stowe MS.* 388.]

63. HENRY ST. JOHN, VISCOUNT BOLINGBROKE. [b. 1678—d. 1751.] Letter to George Clarke, formerly Secretary-at-War, giving his reason for removing from Paris, relying on the good opinion of his friends and "a conscience void of guilt," with which supports "I hope to wade thro' that sea of troubles in to which I have been the first plung'd; tho' I confess I do not see the shore on which one may hope to land." Dated, Belle Vue near Lyons, 27 June, 1715. [*Egerton MS.* 2618, f. 217.]

64. SIR ROBERT WALPOLE. [b. 1676—d. 1745.] Letter, written as First Lord of the Treasury, to the Duke of Newcastle, Secretary of State, respecting action to be taken in regard to the prosecution by the House of Commons of John Huggins, late Warden of the Fleet Prison, for cruelty to prisoners. [A.D. 1730.] *Holograph.* [*Newcastle Papers.*] *Presented, in* 1886, *by the Earl of Chichester.*

65. WILLIAM PITT, afterwards EARL OF CHATHAM. [b. 1708—d. 1778.] Letter to the Duke of Newcastle, First Lord of the Treasury, complaining of the concealment from him of a correspondence between Major Gen. Joseph Yorke, Minister at the Hague, and an unknown lady at Paris, concerning proposals of peace. The letter ends: "I acknowledge my unfitness for the high station where His Majesty has been pleased to place me, but while the King deigns to continue me there, I trust it is not presumption to lay myself at His Majesty's feet and most humbly request his gracious permission to retire, whenever His Majesty thinks it for his service to treat of a Peace in the vehicle of letters of amusement and to order his servants to conceal, under so thin a covering, the first dawnings of information relative to so high and delicate an object." Dated, Hayes, 23 Oct. 1759. *Holograph.* [*Newcastle Papers.*] *Presented, in* 1886, *by the Earl of Chichester.*

66. ROBERT CLIVE, afterwards LORD CLIVE. [b. 1725—d. 1774.] Letter to Warren Hastings, ordering him to wait on the Nabob to receive a lac of rupees, which he had desired him to advance for payment of the troops, and to insist upon the demand being complied with. Dated, Calcutta, 27 Feb. 1759. *Holograph.* [*Add. MS.* 29,131, f. 65.]

67. WARREN HASTINGS, Governor-General of India. [b. 1732—d. 1818.] Letter to his wife, referring to his duel with Mr. (afterwards Sir) Philip Francis; [17 Aug. 1780]. [*Add. MS.* 29,197, f. 14.]

68. EDMUND BURKE. [b. 1730—d. 1797.] Letter to Major-General Hon. John Vaughan, relative to a petition to Parliament from Samuel Hoheb, a Jewish merchant of St. Eustatius, complaining of the seizure of his property on the capture of the island by Gen. Vaughan and Admiral Rodney. [Feb. 1782.] *Holograph.* [*Egerton MS.* 2137, f. 82.]

69. WILLIAM PITT, the younger. [b. 1759—d. 1806]. Letter, as Prime Minister, to the Marquis of Carmarthen, Foreign Secretary, relative to the Convention between England and Spain. Dated, Addiscombe, 21 Nov. 1790. *Holograph.* [*Add. MS.* 27,915, f. 20.]

70. CHARLES JAMES FOX. [b. 1748—d. 1806.] Letter to the Duchess of Leinster, relative to the petition against the bill of attainder of her son Lord Edward Fitzgerald, concluding with the words, "nor can any thing make me have, I will not say a friendly, but even a patient feeling towards the Government of this country, till his poor children are reinstated in their rights." Dated, Holkham, 21 Oct. [1798]. *Holograph.* [*Add. MS.* 30,990, f. 45.]

71. HORATIO, VISCOUNT NELSON. [b. 1758–d. 1805.] Letter written by him on the eve of the battle of Trafalgar, and addressed to Lady Hamilton, telling her that the enemy's combined fleets were coming out of port, and that he hoped to live to finish his letter; dated on board the Victory, 19 Oct. 1805. A postscript, written on the 20th Oct., the day before the battle, was added, as follows: "Oct. 20th. In the morning, we were close to the mouth of the streights, but the wind had not come far enough to the westward to allow the combined fleets to weather the shoals off Trafalgar; but they were counted as far as forty sail of ships of war, which I suppose to be 34 of the Line and six frigates. A group of them was seen off the Lighthouse of Cadiz this morning, but it blows so very fresh and thick weather that I rather believe they will go into the Harbour before night. May God Almighty give

us success over these fellows and enable us to get a Peace." *Holograph.* Below is written, in the hand of Lady Hamilton: "This letter was found open on *his* Desk and brought to Lady Hamilton by Captain Hardy. Oh, miserable wretched Emma! Oh, glorious and happy Nelson!" [*Egerton MS.* 1614.]

Below this letter of Lord Nelson is a small box made from a splinter of the *Victory*, knocked off by a shot in the battle of Trafalgar, and containing a portion of Nelson's hair. *Presented, in* 1865, *by Capt. Wm. Gunton.*

72. SIR ARTHUR WELLESLEY, afterwards DUKE OF WELLINGTON. [b. 1769—d. 1852.] Letter to General Sir Robert Wilson on preparations for the campaign in the Peninsula and the probability of a siege of Ciudad Rodrigo by the French. Dated, Lisbon, 2 Sept. 1809. [*Add. MS.* 30,114, f. 9.]

73. SIR ROBERT PEEL, First Lord of the Treasury. [b. 1788—d. 1850.] Letter to Sir Robert Inglis, on the impossibility of increasing a Civil List pension. Dated, Whitehall, 27 Feb. 1843. *Holograph.* [*Add. MS.* 32,441, f. 379.] *Presented, in* 1884, *by Mrs. A. Bennett.*

74. HENRY JOHN TEMPLE, VISCOUNT PALMERSTON, Secretary of State for Foreign Affairs. [b. 1784—d. 1865.] Letter to R. B. Hoppner, British representative at Lisbon, on the course to be followed in case of an outbreak of hostilities at Lisbon on the landing of Dom Pedro. Dated 18 June, 1832. *Holograph.* [*Egerton MS.* 2343, f. 6.]

75. EDWARD GEOFFREY SMITH STANLEY, EARL OF DERBY, First Lord of the Treasury. [b. 1799—d. 1869.] Letter to the Right Hon. Spencer Horatio Walpole, Home Secretary, on the appointment of the Lord-Lieutenant of Clackmannanshire. Dated 2 July, 1852. *Holograph. Presented, in* 1886, *by the Right Hon. S. H. Walpole.*

75*. BENJAMIN DISRAELI, afterwards EARL OF BEACONSFIELD. [b. 1805—d. 1881.] Letter, written when Chancellor of the Exchequer, to the Right Hon. Spencer Horatio Walpole, Home Secretary, on business in the House of Commons. Dated 29 Nov. 1852. *Holograph. Presented, in* 1886, *by the Right Hon. S. H. Walpole.*

76. Charles George Gordon, Governor-General of the Soudan. [b. 1833—d. 1885.] Letter to his sister, Mary Augusta Gordon: "Kartoum, 27 Feb. [18]84.—I have sent Stewart off to scour the river White Nile, and another expedition to push back rebels on Blue Nile. With Stewart has gone Power, the British Consul and *Times* Correspondent; so I am left *alone* in the vast palace of which you have a photo., but not alone, for I feel great confidence in my Saviour's presence. The peculiar pain which comes from the excessive anxiety one cannot help being in for these peoples comes back to me at times. I think that our Lord sitting over Jerusalem is ruling all things to the glory of His Kingdom, and cannot wish things even different than they are; for if I did do so, then I wish *my will* not *His* be done. The Soudan is a ruin, and humanly speaking there is no hope. Either I must believe He does all things in mercy and love, or else I disbelieve His existence; there is no half-way in the matter. What holes do I not put myself [in]! and for what? So mixed are my ideas. I believe ambition put me here, in this ruin. However, I trust and stay myself on the fact that not one sparrow falls to ground without our Lord's permission, also that enough for the day is its evil. 'God provideth for the way, Strength sufficient for the day.' 1 March.—We are all right at present, and I have hope; but certainly things are not in a good way, humanly speaking. Baker's defeat at Suakin has been a great disaster, and now it has its effects up here. It is nothing to our God to help with many or with few, and I now take my worries more quietly than before. All things are ruled by Him for His glory, and it is rebellion to murmur against His will." *Holograph. Presented, in* 1886, *by Miss Mary Augusta Gordon.*

IV.—HISTORICAL.

[In frames attached to Table L. at the South end of the Room.]

77. HENRY VI. Articles "For ye goode Reule, demesnyng, and seuretee of ye kynges persone and draught of him to vertue and connyng and eschuying of eny thing that mighte yeve empeschement or let therto, or cause any charge, defaulte or blame to be leyd upon ye Erle of Warrewyk [Richard de Beauchamp] at eny tyme withouten his desert": being a series of proposals made by the Earl, as Royal Guardian, to the Privy Council, with their answers to the same; 29 Nov. 11 Henr. VI. [1432]. The king was just completing his eleventh year. The fourth article is to the effect that, as the king's growth in years, in stature and in knowledge of his royal authority "causen him more and more to grucche with chastising and to lothe it," the Earl begs the Council to support him, if necessary, in his chastisements of his kingly pupil, and to bear him scatheless against his anger at such treatment. At the foot of the document are the signatures of the Council; —H[umphrey Plantagenet, Duke of] Gloucester; J[ohn Kemp, Archbishop of] York; P[hilip Morgan, Bishop of] Ely; W[illiam Grey, Bishop of] Lincoln; J[ohn Stafford, Bishop of] Bath, Chancellor; J[ohn Langdon, Bishop of] Rochester; J[ohn Holland, 2nd Earl of] Huntingdon; [William de la Pole, 4th Earl of] Suffolk; and H[umphrey Stafford, 6th Earl of] Stafford. [*Add. Ch.* 17,228.]

78. PERKIN WARBECK, pretended son of Edward IV. Letter to Barnard de la Force, Knt., at Fontarabia, in Spain, desiring him to be his "counseillour and ffrende" as he had been to his father Edw. IV. Dated, Edinburgh, 18 Oct. [1496]. Signed "Your frend RYCHARD OFF ENGLAND." [*Egerton MS.* 616, f. 5.]

79. DECLARATION of Eight Bishops of the Church of England, recognising the authority of Christian princes in Ecclesiastical matters; [1538]. Signed by T[homas Cranmer], Archbishop of Canterbury; Cuthbert [Tunstall], Bishop of Durham; John [Stokesley], Bishop of London; John [Clark], Bishop of Bath and Wells

Thomas [Goodrich], Bishop of Ely; Nicholas [Shaxton], Bishop of Salisbury; Hugh [Latimer], Bishop of Worcester; and J[ohn Hilsey], Bishop of Rochester. [*Stowe MS.* 346.]

80. Edward VI. Letter of the King and his Council to the Bishops, in confirmation of the use of the Book of Common Prayer, and ordering them to collect and "deface and abholish" all Roman Catholic service-books. Dated, Westminster, 25 Dec. aº 3 [1549]. Signed at the top "Edward." [*Stowe MS.* 155.]

81. Queen Elizabeth. Proclamation of the reason of her armament on account of the hostile intentions of the House of Guise and its influence over Mary, Queen of Scots, and her husband, Francis II. of France. The Queen "is content to thinke that the injurious pretense made by the Quene of Scotland to this realme so many maner of wayes hath byn bred and issued only out of the hartes of the principalles of the House of Guise to whom the chief governance of the crowne of France now of late hath happened; and that neither the French king, by reason of his yong yeres, not so capable of suche an enterprise, nor the Quene of Scottes his wief, being also in her minoritie, nor yet the princes of the blud royall and other estates of France . . . . . have imagyned and intended of themselfes suche an unjust, unprobable, and so daungerous an enterprise." [A.D. 1559.] Signed "Elizabeth R." [*Add. Ch.* 16,579.]

82. James VI. of Scotland. Letter to Robert Dudley, Earl of Leicester, congratulating him on his absence from England at the time of "the pretendit condemnation" of his mother, Mary, Queen of Scots, and desiring him to exert his influence that "the rest of this tragedie may be unperfytid." Dated, Holyrood House, 4 Dec. 1586. *Holograph.* [*Add. MS.* 32,092, f. 56.]

83. Henry, Prince of Wales. Letter to his father, James I., sending a list of proposed Knights of the Bath at his creation as Prince of Wales, and asking for leave to go with the Prince of Brunswick to Chatham to see the ships; [May, 1610]. *Holograph.* [*Cotton MS.* Vesp. F. iii., f. 11 b.]

84. Arabella Stuart. Letter to her cousin James I., after her arrest for marrying William Seymour, thanking

him for a relaxation of her imprisonment and begging for his favour: . . . . "And since it hath pleased your Majesty to give this testimony of willingnesse to have me live awhile, in all humility I begge the restitution of those comforts without which every houre of my life is discomfortable to me, the principall whearof is your Majestys favour, which none that breathes can more highely esteeme then I." [A.D. 1610.] *Holograph.* [*Harley MS.* 7003, f. 89.]

85. CHARLES I. Instructions to Sir Edward Herbert, Attorney-General, relative to the impeachment of Lord Kimbolton [Viscount Mandeville] and the Five Members. [3 Jan. 164½]. *Holograph.* It is evident that Mandeville's impeachment was an afterthought, the King having, at first, as appears from the erasures, included his name among the peers whom he intended to call as witnesses. [*Egerton MS.* 2546, f. 20.]

86. CHARLES I. Warrant to Sir Edw. Herbert to desist from further proceedings on the impeachment of Lord Kimbolton and the Five Members. Dated, Theobalds, 3 March, 1641[2]. Signed "CHARLES R." [*Egerton MS.* 2546, f. 21.]

87. CHARLES I. Letter, when prisoner at Carisbrooke, to Henry Firebrace, relative to plans for his escape, etc. Dated 24 July, 1648. Written, partly in cipher, in a feigned hand, speaking of himself in the third person. *Holograph.* [*Egerton MS.* 1788.]

88. QUEEN HENRIETTA MARIA. Letter, in *French*, to Charles I., respecting the supply of ammunition and military movements. Dated, York, 11 May [1643]. *Holograph.* Partly in cipher, with interlinear decipherings by the King. [*Egerton MS.* 2619, f. 18.]

89. OLIVER CROMWELL. Letter to his wife, referring to his daughter Bettie [Elizabeth Claypole] and other members of their family: "I praise the Lord I am encreased in strength in my outward man, but that will not satisfie mee except I gett a heart to love and serve my heavenly Father better and gett more of the light of his countenance, which is better then life, and more power over my corruptions . . . . Minde poore Bettie of the Lords late great mercye. Oh, I desire her not only to seeke the Lord in her necessitye, but indeed and in truth to turne to the Lord and to keepe

closse to him," etc. Dated, [Edinburgh] 12 Apr. 1651. [*Egerton MS.* 2620, f. 9.]

90. GENERAL CHARLES FLEETWOOD. Letter to General George Monck, in "behalfe of that distressed familie of his late Highnes [Oliver Cromwell], whose condicion I thincke is as sad as any poore familie in England, the debts contracted during y^e goverment falling upon my Lord Richard Cromwel." Dated, Wallingford House, 14 Jan. 16$\frac{59}{60}$. Signed. [*Egerton MS.* 2618, f. 58.]

91. RICHARD CROMWELL, late Lord Protector of England. Letter to General George Monck, asking his interest with the Parliament "that I bee not left liable to debts which I am confident neither God nor Conscience can ever reckon mine." Dated 18 Apr. 1660. Signed "R. CROMWELL." [*Egerton MS.* 2618, f. 67.]

92. CHARLES II. Speech to the House of Commons, addressed to the Members in the Banqueting Hall in Whitehall, 1 Mar. 166$\frac{1}{2}$. *Holograph.* [*Egerton MS.* 2546, f. 29.]

93. WILLIAM, PRINCE OF ORANGE [afterwards William III. of England]. Letter, in *French*, to Admiral Arthur Herbert [afterwards Earl of Torrington], announcing the landing of his troops in Torbay and his intention of marching on Exeter, and making arrangements for sending on the baggage to Exmouth. Dated, "Au camp de Torbay," $\frac{6}{16}$ Nov. 1688. *Holograph.* [*Egerton MS.* 2621, f. 39.]

94. WILLIAM, PRINCE OF ORANGE. Questions submitted to him in regard to movements of the Dutch fleet, etc., after the landing in Torbay; with the Prince's directions, in *French*, in the margin. [10 Dec. 1688.] [*Egerton MS.* 2621, f. 73.]

95. WILLIAM III. Instructions to Admiral Arthur Herbert for the disposal of the person of the late King James II., in case of his capture at sea. Dated, Whitehall, 16 March, 168$\frac{8}{9}$. With signatures and seal of William III. and countersignature of [Daniel Finch] Earl of Nottingham, Secretary of State. [*Egerton MS.* 2621, f. 87.]

96. WILLIAM PRYNNE. [b. 1600—d. 1669.] Letter to Thomas, Lord Fairfax, protesting against his imprisonment "with other Members of the Commons House," and demanding "what kinde of Prisoner I am, and

whose?" Dated "from my Prison at the Kings-head in the Strand," 3 Jan. $164\frac{8}{9}$. *Holograph.* [*Egerton MS.* 2618, f. 31.]

97. ALGERNON SIDNEY. [b. 1622—d. 1683.] Letter, when Ambassador in Denmark, to Bulstrode Whitelocke, on the conduct of the English Parliament and the movements of General Monck. Dated, Elsinore, 13 Nov. [1659]. *Holograph.* [*Add. MS.* 32,093, f. 416.]

98. JOHN GRAHAM, OF CLAVERHOUSE, afterwards VISCOUNT OF DUNDEE. [b. 1650—d. 1689.] Letter to [George Livingston] Earl of Linlithgow, Commander-in-Chief in Scotland, giving an account of the skirmish with the Covenanters at Drumclog: "We keeped our fyr till they wer within ten pace of us; they received our fyr and advanced to the shok. The first they gave us broght doun the coronet, Mr. Crafford, and Captain Bleith . . . . which so disincoroged our men that they sustined not the shok but fell into disorder. There horse took the occasion of this and persecud us so hotly that we got no tym to ragly. I saved the standarts, but lost on the place about aight ord ten men, beseids wounded; but the dragoons lost many mor." Dated, Glasgow, 1 June, 1679. *Holograph.* [*Stowe MS.* 318.]

99. GILBERT BURNET, afterwards BISHOP OF SALISBURY. [b. 1643—d. 1715.] Letter to Admiral Arthur Herbert [afterwards Earl of Torrington], written while accompanying the Prince of Orange on his march from Torbay to London during the Revolution, and giving details of public events, of the desertion of the King by the Princess of Denmark and others, of the arrival of Commissioners to treat with the Prince, etc. Dated, Hungerford, 9 Dec. 1688. *Holograph.* [*Egerton MS.* 2621, f. 69.]

100. ROBERT HARLEY, afterwards EARL OF OXFORD. [b. 1661—d. 1724.] Letter to George Louis, Elector of Hanover [afterwards George I. of England], announcing the removal of the Duchess of Marlborough from the Queen's service. Dated $\frac{19}{30}$ Jan. $171\frac{0}{1}$. *Holograph.* [*Stowe MS.* 388.]

101. SARAH CHURCHILL, DUCHESS OF MARLBOROUGH. [b. 1660—d. 1744.] Letter to James Craggs [afterwards Secretary of State] on her dismissal from Court: "The message the Queen sent me that I might take a lodging for

ten shillings a week to put my Lord Marlboroughs goods in, sufficiently shews what a good education and understanding the wolf has who was certainly the person that gave that advise." [April, 1710.] *Holograph.* [*Stowe MS.* 110.]

102. JOHN WILKES. [b. 1727—d. 1797.] Letter to the Rev. Charles Churchill, the poet, asking him to conduct the "North Briton" for three weeks during his absence, and suggesting subjects for treatment. Dated 25 March [1763]. *Holograph.* [*Add. MS.* 30,878, f. 25.]

103. "JUNIUS." The "Dedication to the English Nation," in the hand of Junius, of Woodfall's first edition of the Collected Letters of Junius, 1772. *Holograph.* [*Add. MS.* 27,775, f. 15.]

V.—LITERARY.

[In frames attached to Table M. at the South end of the Room.]

104. WILLIAM CAMDEN, Clarenceux King of Arms. [b. 1551 —d. 1623.] Letter to Sir Henry Spelman, sending complimentary letters from Nicolas Peiresc and other French scholars on the subject of Spelman's Glossary. Dated, Chislehurst, 19 Sept. 1619. *Holograph.* [*Add. MS.* 25,384, f. 5.]

105. DR. JOHN DONNE, Dean of St. Paul's. [b. 1573— d. 1631.] Letter to Sir Nicholas Throckmorton-Carew, thanking him for his favours and inquiring, on behalf of the Earl of Dorset, at what time a stag will be most acceptable to him. Dated, "at my house at S. Paul's," 1 Sept. 1624. *Holograph.* [*Add. MS.* 29,598, f. 13.]

106. JEREMY TAYLOR, Bishop of Down and Connor. [b. 1613 —d. 1667.] Letter to Christopher Hatton, Lord Hatton: will send over in the spring the tracts D[uctor] D[ubitantium], etc.; the king has forgiven the Irish clergy their first fruits and twentieths, and sends over a lieutenant who will excel the Earl of Strafford in his kindness to the church. Dated, Dublin, 23 Nov. 1661. *Holograph.* [*Add. MS.* 29,584, f. 6.]

107. SAMUEL PEPYS, Secretary of the Admiralty. [b. 1632 —d. 1703.] Letter to — Reeves, on business connected

with Christ's Hospital. Dated 9 April, 1694. *Holograph.* [*Add. MS.* 20,732, f. 8.]

108. George Fox, the Quaker [d. 1690.] Explanation of "Arones linen breches" and other types from the Old Testament. *Holograph.* [*Stowe MS.* 709.]

109. Richard Baxter, the Nonconformist. [b. 1615—d. 1691.] Portion of a narrative of passages of his life and times, relating to proceedings at the beginning of the Long Parliament; published in *Reliquiæ Baxterianæ*, 1695. *Holograph.* [*Egerton MS.* 2570, f. 1.]

110. George Whitefield, the Methodist. [b. 1714—d. 1770.] Letter addressed to "My dear brethren in Christ," on differences of gifts and graces, on separation from the Church of England, etc. Dated, Bristol, 28 Dec. 1741. *Holograph.* [*Add. MS.* 29,960 B., f. 13.]

111. John Wesley. [b. 1703—d. 1791.] Letter to "Mr. Richard Burke, at the Preaching house, in Waterford," explaining his inability at present to assist him, living himself "as we say, from hand to mouth," and thinking "it very hard if Ireland cannot allow a maintenance to the preachers in Ireland," etc. Dated, Edinburgh, 12 May, 1770. *Holograph.* [*Add. MS.* 29,300, f. 68.]

112. Samuel Richardson, the Novelist. [b. 1689—d. 1761.] Letter to [Cox Macro, D.D,], in defence of "the compromise between Sir Charles Grandison and Clementina in the article of religion." Dated, Salisbury Court, Fleet Street, 22 March, 1754. *Holograph.* [*Add. MS.* 32,557, f. 176.]

113. Laurence Sterne. [b. 1713—d. 1768.] Letter to [T. Becket, his publisher], respecting books to be sent to Denis Diderot in France, and business matters connected with the sale of "Tristram Shandy." Dated, Paris, 12 [April?], 1762. [*Egerton MS.* 1662, f. 5.]

114. Oliver Goldsmith. [b. 1728—d. 1774.] Agreement (never carried out) to write for James Dodsley, the publisher, a "Chronological History of the Lives of eminent persons of Great Britain and Ireland," at the rate of 3 guineas a sheet. Dated 31 March, 1763. In Goldsmith's handwriting, and signed by both parties. [*Add. MS.* 19,022, f. 8.] *Presented, in* 1852, *by Samuel Rogers, Esq.*

115. Dr. Samuel Johnson. [b. 1709—d. 1784.] Note, on

a card, to John Wilkes and his daughter, in answer to an invitation. Dated 24 May, 1783. *Holograph.* [*Add. MS.* 30,877, f. 97.]

116. JAMES BOSWELL. [b. 1740—d. 1795.] Note to John Wilkes and his daughter, enclosing Dr. Johnson's card as above, and regretting that "so agreable a meeting must be deferred till next year." Dated, South Audley Street, 25 May [1783]. *Holograph.* [*Add. MS.* 30,877, f. 97.]

117. DAVID GARRICK. [b. 1716—d. 1779.] Letter to Woodfall the publisher, complaining of a criticism on Bate's farce "The Blackamoor washed white." Dated 13 [Feb. 1776]. *Holograph.* [*Add. MS.* 21,508, f. 31.]

118. JOHN PHILIP KEMBLE. [b. 1757—d. 1823.] Letter to Samuel Ireland, desiring him to send the manuscript of the play of "Vortigern" [alleged to be by Shakespeare]. Dated 27 Dec. 1795. *Holograph.* [*Add. MS.* 30,348, f. 62.]

119. SARAH SIDDONS. [b. 1755—d. 1831.] Letter to Samuel Ireland, regretting her inability through illness to act in "Vortigern." [29 March, 1796.] *Holograph.* [*Add. MS.* 30,348, f. 93.]

120. EDMUND KEAN. [b. 1787—d. 1833.] Letter to R. Philips, apologising for an insult offered to him under his roof, etc. Dated 5 June [1829]. *Holograph.* [*Egerton MS.* 2159, f. 89.]

121. JOHN FLAXMAN. [b. 1754—d. 1826.] Letter to William Hayley on a design for a monument for Capt. Quantock in Chichester Cathedral, and on differences between W. Hayley and his wife. Dated 14 Feb. 1813. *Holograph.* [*Add. MS.* 30,805, f. 42.]

122. SIR DAVID WILKIE, R.A. [b. 1785—d. 1841.] Letter to Perry Nursey, giving news of various artists, and stating that the copies for the English market of the new novel "Ivan-Hoe," by the "great unknown," which "is said to be a very fine thing," are reported to have been lost at sea. Dated, Kensington, 28 Dec. 1819. *Holograph.* [*Add. MS.* 29,991, f. 22.]

123. JOSEPH MALLORD WILLIAM TURNER, R.A. [b. 1775—d. 1851.] Letter to Dawson Turner, of Yarmouth, thanking him for a present of bloaters; Mr. Phillips is recovering; is sorry to see by the paper that Sir A. W.

Callcott, R.A., is dead, and that a robbery has been committed on the bank of Samuel Rogers. Dated 26 Nov. 1844. *Holograph.* [*Add. MS.* 29,960 B.]

124. Thomas Gray. [b. 1716—d. 1771.] A fair copy of the "Elegy, written in a country churchyard"; enclosed in a letter to Dr. Thomas Wharton. Dated, Cambridge, 18 Dec. [1750]. *Holograph.* [*Egerton MS.* 2400, f. 45.]

125. Robert Burns. [b. 1759—d. 1796.] Song, "Here's a health to them that's awa." *Holograph.* [*Egerton MS.* 1656, f. 27.]

126. John Keats. [b. 1795—d. 1821.] Letter to James Elmes, concerning some verses, which "can be struck out in no time," for Haydon, the painter. Dated, Wentworth Place, Hampstead [*circ.* 1818]. *Holograph.* [*Add. MS.* 22,130, f. 91.]

127. Percy Bysshe Shelley. [b. 1792—d. 1822.] Letter to Miss Curran, at Rome, concerning designs for a monument, and mentioning that he has nearly finished his "Cenci" and wishes "to get a good engraving made of the picture in the Colonna Palace." Dated, Livorno, 5 Aug. 1819. *Holograph.* [*Add. MS.* 22,130, f. 94.]

128. Robert Southey. [b. 1774—d. 1843.] Letter to his brother, Capt. Thomas Southey, R.N., concerning a "tender epistle to Brougham" in answer to an attack upon him by Brougham from the hustings. Dated 11 July [1818]. *Holograph.* [*Add. MS.* 30,927, f. 266.]

129. Samuel Taylor Coleridge. [b. 1772—d. 1834]. Letter to Basil Montague, concerning the doctrines of Edward Irving, etc. [1 Feb. 1826.] *Holograph.* [*Add. MS.* 21,508, f. 55.]

130. William Wordsworth. [b. 1770—d. 1850]. Letter to Frederic Reynolds, informing him of the benefit derived from the application of "Blue Stone" to his eyes, as Reynolds had advised. Dated, Halsteads, near Penrith, 24 Oct. [1826?]. *Holograph.* [*Add. MS.* 27,925, f. 109.]

131. Charles Lamb. [b. 1775—d. 1834.] Letter to John Clare, thanking him for a present of his poems and criticising his use of provincial phrases; with a recipe for cooking frogs, "the nicest little rabbity things you ever tasted." Dated, India House, 31 Aug. 1822. *Holograph.* [*Egerton MS.* 2246, f. 99.]

132. Sydney Smith. [b. 1771—d. 1845.] Letter to Sir Robert Peel, in answer to an attack upon him for his "interference with the arbitrary proceedings of Railroads": a communication to the "Morning Chronicle," 20 June, 1842. *Holograph.* [*Add. MS.* 29,300, f. 102.]

133. Thomas Hood. [b. 1798—d. 1845.] Letter to Sir E. Bulwer Lytton, concerning an article written by the latter for his Magazine, and a report that he had "taken leave of authorship." Dated 30 Oct. 1844. *Holograph.* [*Add. MS.* 30,262, f. 91.]

134. Theodore Hook. [b. 1788—d. 1841.] Humorous Letter to Thomas Aston Baylis, in answer to a complaint of the destruction by his servant of a cat belonging to Mrs. Baylis; *n. d.* *Holograph.* [*Egerton MS.* 2264, f. 10.]

135. Edward Bulwer Lytton, Lord Lytton. [b. 1805—d. 1873.] Letter to William Charles Mark Kent (better known as Charles Kent), on his being gazetted to the peerage: "You are the first to whom I doff my baptismal initials and sign myself Lytton." [14 July, 1866.] *Holograph.* [*Add. MS.* 32,645.] *Presented, in* 1886, *by Charles Kent, Esq.*

136. Charles Dickens. [b. 1812—d. 1870.] Letter written the day before his death to Charles Kent, appointing to meet him on the morrow: "To-morrow is a very bad day for me to make a call . . . . but I hope I may be ready for you at 3 o'clock. If I can't be—why then I shan't be. You must really get rid of those opal enjoyments. They are too overpowering. 'These violent delights have violent ends.' I think it was a father of your church who made the wise remark to a young gentleman who got up early (or stayed out late) at Verona." Dated, Gad's Hill Place, 8 June, 1870. *Holograph.* [*Add. MS.* 31,022, f. 1.] *Presented, in* 1879, *by Charles Kent, Esq.*

---

137. George Frederick Handel. [b. 1684—d. 1759.] Portion of the original manuscript of the anthem "As pants the hart." *Holograph.* [*Add. MS.* 30,308, f. 130.]

138. George Frederick Handel. [b. 1684—d. 1759.] Letter to [the Keeper of the Ordnance Office], requesting him to deliver the artillery kettle-drums lent to him for

use in his oratorios. Dated 24 Feb. 1750. *Holograph.* [*Add. MS.* 24,182, f. 15.]

139. JOSEPH HAYDN. [b. 1732—d. 1809.] Letter, in *German*, to William Forster, musical instrument maker, complaining of Artaria, the music publisher of Vienna, and mentioning the enhanced value of his compositions and that he had a contract for six pieces for upwards of 100 guineas. Dated, Esterhazy, 28 Feb. 1788. *Holograph.* [*Egerton MS.* 2380, f. 9.]

140. LUDWIG VAN BEETHOVEN. [b. 1770—d. 1827.] Letter, in *German*, to Baron Ignaz von Gleichenstein, with reference to a change in the dedication of one of his works; [1808?] *Holograph.* [*Add. MS.* 29,804, f. 10.]

141. FRANZ SCHUBERT. [b. 1797—d. 1828.] Letter, in *German*, to Anselm Hüttenbrenner, of Grätz, begging him to use his interest to secure for his brother Karl a post as teacher of drawing at Grätz; with an account of the performance of a new trio. Dated, Vienna, 18 Jan. 1828. *Holograph.* [*Add. MS.* 29,804, f. 24.]

142. FELIX MENDELSSOHN-BARTHOLDY. [b. 1809—d. 1847.] Testimonial in favour of George Hogarth, the musical critic. Dated, Leipzig, July, 1838. *Holograph.* [*Egerton MS.* 2159, f. 95.]

143. JOHANN WOLFGANG VON GOETHE. [b. 1749—d. 1832.] Letter in *German*, to ——, giving reasons for not entering at length upon a discussion of "die Windischmannische Recension," and returning his correspondent's manuscript. Dated, Weimar, 4 Aug. 1811. *Holograph.* [*Egerton MS.* 2407, f. 122.]

144. JOHANN CHRISTOPH FRIEDRICH VON SCHILLER. [b. 1759 —d. 1805.] Letter, in *German*, to [Karl Theodor Körner] on domestic matters, with remarks upon C. F. Zelte's satisfactory setting of his ballad "Der Taucher" to music, upon F. Schlegel's tragedy "Alarcos" and Goethe's support of it, and upon W. Schlegel's tragedy "Ion." Dated, Weimar, 5 July, 1802. *Holograph.* [*Add. MS.* 29,804, f. 3.]

VI.—LITERARY WORKS, ETC.

[In the cases on the South-west side of the Room; and in those adjoining at right angles, as the visitor advances towards the Grenville Room.]

145. HENRY VIII. Metrical version of the Penitential and other Psalms, in *English;* written early in the 16th century. With a portrait of Henry VIII. Bound in gold, worked in open leaf-tracery. At the top of the covers are rings to attach the volume to the girdle. [*Stowe MS.* 153.]

146. EDWARD VI. Treatise on the Sacrament of the Body and Blood of Christ, in *French*, composed in 1549 by King Edward VI., and in his handwriting; with corrections by his tutor. [*Add. MS.* 29,432.]

147. EDWARD SEYMOUR, DUKE OF SOMERSET. A small volume containing the Calendar, and various tables for the moveable feasts, epacts, etc.; and having on the fly-leaf some Scriptural verses written by the Duke of Somerset the day before his execution, which took place on the 22nd Jan. 155½. [*Stowe MS.* 154.]

148. LADY JANE GREY. A small Manual of Prayers in English, written on vellum, with miniatures; believed to have been used by Lady Jane Grey on the scaffold, 12 Feb. 155¾. It contains on the margins, some lines in the handwriting of Lady Jane, addressed to Sir John Gage, Lieutenant of the Tower, and to the Duke of Suffolk, her father. [*Harley MS.* 2342.]

149. ELIZABETH, WHEN PRINCESS. Prayers or Meditations, composed originally in *English* by Queen Katherine Parr, and translated into *Latin*, *French*, and *Italian*, by Queen Elizabeth, when Princess. Entirely in her own handwriting, on vellum, with a dedication to her father, King Henry VIII.; dated from Hertford, 20 Dec. 1545. In a silk binding, embroidered with silver. [*Royal MS.* 7 D. x.]

150. MARY, QUEEN OF SCOTS. The Original Draft, in *French*, of the Will of Mary, Queen of Scots, partly in the handwriting of Nau, her Secretary, but with corrections and many additions in the handwriting of the

Queen; dated at Sheffield Manor [in Yorkshire], February, 1577. [*Cotton MS.* Vesp. C. xvi.]

151. CHARLES I., WHEN PRINCE. "FLORUM FLORES, sive Florum ex veterum Poetarum floribus excerptorum Flores"; a selection of passages from the Classical Latin Poets, entirely in the handwriting of Prince Charles, and presented by him to his father James I. as a new year's gift. [*Royal MS.* 12 D. viii.]

152. JAMES, DUKE OF MONMOUTH. [b. 1649—d. 1685.] Memorandum-Book of James [Scott], Duke of Monmouth [natural son of Charles II.], almost wholly in his handwriting. [*Egerton MS.* 1527.]

153. CARDINAL WOLSEY. [b. 1471—d. 1530.] The Life of Cardinal Wolsey, by George Cavendish, his Gentleman Usher. The original MS. [*Egerton MS.* 2402.]

154. WILLIAM CECIL, LORD BURGHLEY. Memorandum-book of public and private business, *circ.* 1592. [*Royal MS.* Appx. 67.]

155. JAMES I. ΒΑΣΙΛΙΚΟΝ ΔΩΡΟΝ, or Book of the Institution of a Prince; written by King James for the instruction of his son, Prince Henry; wholly in the King's handwriting. In the original binding of crimson velvet, with the King's initials and the arms of Scotland, in gold. [*Royal MS.* 18 B. xv.]

156. BEN JONSON. "The Masque of Queenes," represented at Whitehall, 2 Feb. 1609. In the autograph of the author, with a dedicatory address to Prince Henry. [*Royal MS.* 18 A. xiv.]

157. SIR FRANCIS BACON. Memorandum-book of Sir Francis Bacon, afterwards Lord Verulam, containing memoranda for his conduct in public and private business, literary notes, etc., entered in July and August, 1608. [*Add. MS.* 27,278.]

158. JOHN MILTON. Album Amicorum of Christopher Arnold, Professor of History at Nuremberg, containing autographs collected in the years 1649–1672; including a sentence in Greek, signed by the Poet Milton, "JOANNES MILTONIUS," and dated London, 19 Nov. 1651. [*Egerton MS.* 1324.]

159. PERCY BALLADS. The volume of English Ballads and Romances, from which Bishop Percy selected the poems published under the title of "Reliques of Ancient

English Poetry"; written in the middle of the 17th century. [*Add. MS.* 27,879.]

160. "A Testimonie of Antiquitie, shewing the auncient fayth in the Church of England touching the Sacrament of the Body and Bloude of the Lord": a printed book [1567]. It contains an Anglo-Saxon homily by Ælfric, accompanied by a translation, at the end of which is an attestation of its fidelity by seventeen Archbishops and Bishops of England, with their signatures, amongst them being: Matthew [Parker], Archbishop of Canterbury, Thomas [Young], Archbishop of York, Edmund [Grindal], Bishop of London, James [Pilkington], Bishop of Durham, Robert [Horne], Bishop of Winchester, William [Barlow], Bishop of Chichester, John [Scory], Bishop of Hereford, Richard [Cox], Bishop of Ely, Edwin [Sandys], Bishop of Worcester, [Nicholas Bullingham], Bishop of Lincoln. [*Add. MS.* 18,160.] *Presented, in* 1850, *by William Maskell, Esq.*

161. John Milton. [b. 1608—d. 1674.] The Holy Bible: printed by Robert Barker, London, 1612. The copy which formerly belonged to John Milton, who has entered, in his own hand, on a blank page, memoranda of the births, etc., of himself and members of his family; others being added by a different hand under Milton's direction. [*Add. MS.* 32,310.]

162. Lionardo da Vinci. Book of observations and demonstrations on subjects chiefly of mixed mathematics, being unconnected notes entered at different times, beginning 22 March, 1508. Written in his own hand from right to left in reversed letters. [*Arundel MS.* 263.]

163. Torquato Tasso. [b. 1544—d. 1595.] The autograph manuscript of his Tragedy intitled "Torismondo," with numerous corrections. From the Library of Cardinal Cibo. [*Add. MS.* 23,778.]

164. Lope Felix de Vega Carpio. Comedies, in *Spanish*, in the author's handwriting, A.D. 1624–1628. The volume is open at the end of the Third Act of "Sin secreto no ai Amor," showing the poet's signature, and the licence for the piece to be acted, dat. 13 Dec. 1626. [*Egerton MS.* 548.]

165. Frederic II., King of Prussia. A volume containing various writings of Frederic II., sent to Andrew

Mitchell, when Ambassador at the Court of Berlin, in 1756–1763. Among these papers is the one entitled, "*Reflexions sur les talents militaires de Charles XII. Roy de Suede*," entirely in the King's handwriting. [*Add. MS.* 6845.]

166. JEAN JACQUES ROUSSEAU. "Rousseau juge de Jean Jacques": the first of the three Dialogues composed by Rousseau, in justification of his own writings. The present copy is in his handwriting, and was given by him on the 6th of April, 1776, to Brooke Boothby, Esq., who presented it to the British Museum, in 1781. [*Add. MS.* 4925.]

167. WILLIAM HARVEY. Original notes for Lectures on Universal Anatomy, delivered on 16, 17 and 18 April, 1616. [*Sloane MS.* 230.]

168. JOHN LOCKE. Original Diary and Note-Book kept by John Locke, during the year 1679, partly whilst at Paris, and partly in England. [*Add. MS.* 15,642.]

169. LUCY HUTCHINSON. Original MS. of the Memoirs of Colonel John Hutchinson, M.P., Governor of Nottingham [d. 1664], by his widow, Lucy, daughter of Sir A. Apsley. [*Add. MS.* 25,901.]

170. ALEXANDER POPE. [b. 1688—d. 1744.] A volume of the original draft of Pope's Translation of the Iliad and Odyssey in his own handwriting, and for the most part written upon the backs of letters addressed to himself. [*Add. MS.* 4808.] *Presented, in* 1766, *by Mrs. Lucy Mallet.*

171. THOMAS CHATTERTON. [b. 1752—d. 1770.] "Eclogues and other Poems, by Thomas Rowley, with a glossary and annotations by Thomas Chatterton": being a portion of the literary forgeries of Chatterton, in his own handwriting. [*Add. MS.* 24,890.]

172. DANIEL DEFOE. "The Compleat English Gentleman": the original MS. of an unpublished work by Daniel Defoe, written about the year 1729. [*Add. MS.* 32,555.]

173. LAURENCE STERNE. The first part of the corrected draft of "A Sentimental Journey through France and Italy," by Laurence Sterne, M.A. [1767]; in the author's handwriting. [*Egerton MS.* 1610.]

174. DR. SAMUEL JOHNSON. Original draft of Dr. Johnson's Tragedy of "Irene," acted at Drury Lane in 1749; in the author's handwriting. [*King's MS.* 306.]

175. ROBERT BURNS. Autobiography of Robert Burns in a letter addressed to Dr. John Moore; dated, Mauchline, 2 Aug. 1787; with a postscript dated, Edinburgh, 23 Sept. of the same year. The original MS. [*Egerton MS.* 1660.]

176. ROBERT SOUTHEY. [b. 1774—d. 1843.] "Joan of Arc": a poem, in ten books by Robert Southey. The original MS., with notes and corrections for the first edition by the author and S. T. Coleridge. [*Add. MS.* 28,096.]

177. SAMUEL TAYLOR COLERIDGE. [b. 1772—d. 1834.] Memorandum-book, containing fragments of poems, miscellaneous notes, a list of his works, *etc.* [*Add. MS.* 27,901.]

178. SIR WALTER SCOTT. Autograph manuscript of the novel of "Kenilworth," by Sir Walter Scott, corrected for the press; written between Sept. 1820 and Jan. 1821. [*Egerton MS.* 1661.]

179. GEORGE GORDON, LORD BYRON. "Childe Harold's Pilgrimage: a Romaunt." The first and second cantos, as copied for the press for the first edition, London, 1812; with corrections and notes in the author's own hand. [*Egerton MS.* 2027.]

180. THOMAS BABINGTON MACAULAY, LORD MACAULAY. [b. 1800—d. 1859.] A leaf of the rough autograph draft of the twenty-fifth and concluding chapter of his History of England. [*Add. MS.* 24,094.] *Presented, in* 1861, *by his sister, Lady Trevelyan.*

CHARTERS.

[In cases on the right hand, as the visitor enters from the Grenville Library.]

1. Grant, with the consent of ELFRED [ALFRED THE GREAT], King of Wessex, and the Witenagemot, by Archbishop Ethered and the monastery of Christ Church, Canterbury, to Liaba or Leafa, son of Birgwin, of land called Gilding [Yalding?, co. Kent] for 20 [altered into 25] mancuses of gold. Dated A.D. 873. *Latin.* A contemporary copy, in the hand used by Wessex scribes. The

names of the witnesses, which include Æðelulf, King of Wessex [d. 857], and Archbishop Ceolnoth [d. 870], have evidently been copied from other charters. [*Stowe Ch.* 18.]

2. Grant by King EADRED to Ælfwyn, a nun, of six "mansæ," or in the Kentish tongue "syx sulunga," of land at Wicham [Wickham Breaux, co. Kent], for two pounds of the purest gold. Dated A.D. 948. *Latin*, with the boundaries of the land in *Anglo-Saxon.* Witnessed by King Eadred, Eadgifu his mother, Oda, Archbishop of Canterbury, Wulfstan, Archbishop of York, and others. [*Stowe Ch.* 25.]
3. Grant by King CNUT to Bishop Eadsin of land for half a plough (terram dimidii aratri) in East Kent "æt Berwican" [Berwick, co. Kent]. Dated A.D. 1035. *Latin*, with the boundaries in *Anglo-Saxon.* Witnessed by "Cnut rex Anglorum," Æþelnoð, Archbishop of Canterbury, and others. [*Stowe Charter*, 34.]
4. Grant from Hugh Talebot, with the assent of Ermentrude his wife and Gerard, Geoffrey, Hugh and Richard his sons, to the Abbey of St. Mary and St. Laurence of Beaubec, in Normandy, of his land of Fautewella [Feltwell, co. Norf.], from which Aeliza de Cokefelt and Adam her son paid him yearly 100 shillings. Dated A.D. 1165. *Latin.* With seal. [*Harley Ch.* 112, D. 57.]
5. Confirmation by King STEPHEN of a grant from Ilbert de Carencin to Sawtrey Abbey, co. Huntingdon, of land at Gamlingay, co. Cambridge. Witnesses: William, Count of Albemarle, Earl Simon [ex-Earl of Northampton], and others. Dated, Northampton [1146–1151]. *Latin.* [*Harley Ch.* 83 A. 24.]
6. Charter of HENRY II., confirming to the Priory of Bromfield, co. Salop, the church of Bromfield, with the lands and vills of Haverford [Halford], Dodinghopa [Dinchope], Esseford [Ashford], Felton, etc.; granted on the reconstitution of the Priory under the Benedictine Order in 1155. *Latin.* [*Cotton Ch.* XVII. 4.]
7. Grant from Robert [Trianel], Prior, and the Priory of St. Andrew at Northampton, to Christian, Abbat, and the Abbey of Aunay in the diocese of Bayeux in Normandy, of two parts of the tithage of the Lordship of Aissebi [Ashby-Mears, co. Northampton], the Abbey in return paying yearly to the Priory six measures of

winnowed corn into the Priory Grange at Ashby. Witnessed by six priests, three from either House. Dated A.D. 1176. *Latin.* [*Harley Ch.* 44 A. 1.]

8. Agreement whereby the Knights Hospitallers of St. John of Jerusalem surrender to Richard [Toclive], Bishop of Winchester, the charge and administration of the Hospital of St. Cross without the walls of Winchester, the Bishop raising the number of poor there entertained from 113 to 213 (of whom 200 were to be fed and 13 fed and clothed), assigning to the Knights Hospitallers the churches of Morduna [Mordon, co. Surr.] and Haninctona [Hannington, co. Hants], and releasing them from the yearly payment to the monks of St. Swithin of 10 marks and two candles of 10 lbs. of wax. Dated, Dover, 10 Apr. 1185, in the presence of King Henry II., Eraclius Patriarch of Jerusalem, and others. *Latin.* With autograph signatures of Bishop Toclive and Roger de Molins, Master of the Hospital of St. John of Jerusalem. Appended are the leaden "bulla" of R. de Molins, and the seals of the Bishop and of Garnerius de Neapoli, Prior of the Hospitallers in England. [*Harley Ch.* 43 I. 48.]

9. Inspeximus by J[ordan de Villa] Abbat of Thornton, R[ichard] Abbat of Grimsby, A[karius] Abbat of Barlings and W[alter] Prior of Thornholm, of charters in the hands of the Prior of Elsham, co. Lincoln, granted by the family of Amundevill. [A.D. 1203–1205.] *Latin.* [*Harley Ch.* 45 A. 4.]

10. Lease from Juliana, widow of John Frusselov, to Robert, Abbat of Abingdon, and the convent of the same, of all her dower-lands in Dumbelton [Dumbleton, co. Glouc.] for 10 years from "Hocke dai" [2nd Tuesday after Easter], 14 Hen. III. [1230]. Witnesses: Henry de Tracy, Richard, Dean of Dumbleton, etc. [A.D. 1230.] *Latin.* [*Harley Ch.* 75 F. 36.]

11. Assignment by R., Prior of Sempringham, to the nuns of Bullington, co. Lincoln, with the assent of Prior William and the convent of the same, of a yearly rent of five marks for buying their smocks, "ad camisias illarum inperpetuum emendas," issuing from land in Friskney, etc., co. Linc. Dated A.D. 1235. *Latin.* [*Harley Ch.* 44 I. 14.]

12. Agreement between William, Lord of Melebery Os-

mund [Melbury Osmond, co. Dorset], and John Picot, whereby they mutually renounce the right of pasture on each other's lands in Melebery, etc. Witnesses: Sir William son of Henry, Sir William Maubanc, Sir Benedict de Bere, Knts., Sir Richard, vicar of Gateministre [Yeatminster], etc. Dated, St. Margaret's day [20 July], 27 Hen. III. [1243]. *Latin.* [*Harley Ch.* 53 D. 36.]

13. Letter from PHILIPPA, Queen of Edward III. to an English envoy about to proceed to the Papal Court, to bring about a reconciliation between Maistre Wauter Skrillowe a perpetual resident at Rome [Archdeacon of the East Riding of York, in 1370, and afterwards Bishop successively of Lichfield and Coventry, Bath and Wells, and Durham] and her clerk and secretary Sire Johan de Hermesthorp [Archdeacon of the East Riding in 1364], to whom the King had lately given a benefice, which grant is the cause of their strife. Dated, Canterbury, 3 June [1364]. *French.* Presumed to be in the handwriting of William of Wykeham, then Royal Secretary. [*Add. Ch.* 15,422.]

14. Articles of Liberties, demanded by the Barons of King John, and embodied in MAGNA CARTA. *Latin.* An autotype copy of the original preserved in the Department and presented, in 1769, by Philip, Earl Stanhope. A portion of the Great Seal remains. [*Add. MS.* 4838.] A printed copy of the text is placed with it.*

15. Charter of confirmation by ALFONSO the Wise, King of Castile, of royal grants to the hospital near the monastery of Santa Maria Real in Burgos; dated at Burgos, 30 December, era 1292 [A.D. 1254], in which year, it is added, Edward, eldest son and heir of Henry (the third) King of England, received knighthood from King Alfonso in Burgos. *Spanish.* Subscribed with a cross for the royal signature, surrounded by the inscription, "Signo del Rey Don Alfonso," and by the confirmation of Don Juan Garcia, in concentric circles, and attested by the Moorish kings of Granada, Murcia, and Niebla, and by seventy-seven prelates and noblemen. The numerous witnesses were assembled, no doubt, to cele-

* The autotype copy and the printed text can be purchased in the British Museum.

brate the marriage of Eleanor, the King of Castile's sister, with EDWARD, son of Henry the Third of England, afterwards King Edward I., who, as it appears, was knighted by Alfonso on the occasion. The royal seal, impressed on lead, is appended. [*Add. Ch.* 24,804.]

16. Roundel of copper, 9½ inches in circumference, of the 13th century, described, in the memorandum attached to it, as the model of the tonsure of the "officiarii" of St. Paul's Church, London. The vellum label is injured by the fire which took place in the Cottonian Library in 1731. [*Cotton Ch.* xvi. 73.]

17. Grant of indulgence from Friars John Seyvill and William Hullis of the Order of St. John of Jerusalem, as Proctors of Pope Alexander V., to Sir William Fitz Hugh, Knight, and Margery his wife, in consideration of their contributions to the refortifying of the Castle of St. Peter at Budrum, lately captured from the infidels. Dated at Clerkenwell Priory, A.D. 1414. *Latin.* [*Cotton Ch.* iv. 31.]

18. Bull of Pope Eugenius IV., granting permission to the Provost and officials of the New College of Eton to lease out the lands lately bestowed on them, and to receive the rents therefrom and to apply them to the uses of the College. Dated, Florence, Kalends of February, [1 Febr.] A.D. 1445. *Latin.* [*Add. Ch.* 15,570.]

MANUSCRIPTS.

[In the Cases A—F, which occupy the middle of the room, is exhibited a series of MSS., in European and Oriental languages, with the view of illustrating the progress of handwriting. Case A contains Greek MSS. (Nos. 1–22), commencing with works written on papyrus, and showing the course of writing in *uncial*, or large, letters, and the later *minuscule*, or small, letters; from the 2nd century before Christ to A.D. 1479. In Cases B and C are arranged MSS., chiefly in Latin (Nos. 23–96), in which the development of the writing of Western Europe can be followed, from about A.D. 600 to the end of the 15th century. The earliest specimens are written in *uncial*, or large letters, which differ from ordinary capitals chiefly in the rounded forms of A, D, E, H, M (ᴀ, ᴅ, ᴇ, ʜ, ᴍ). To these succeed various specimens of national handwritings in *half-uncial*, or mixed large and small, letters, or *minuscules*, as practised in England, Ireland, France, Italy, and Spain, until in the 9th century the Caroline or Carlovingian form of *minuscule* writing, which developed in the French schools established under the rule of Charlemagne, gradually superseded them, and became the common hand of Western Europe which survives to the present day; as may be seen in the specimens numbered 42 and onwards. Case D contains Anglo-Saxon and English MSS. (Nos. 97–121) from about A.D. 1000 to the 15th century, written in Saxon characters and the succeeding forms of English writing. In Case E are early specimens of Oriental writing; and in Case F, Oriental MSS. of more recent periods.]

I.—GREEK MSS.

Case A.

1. Petition from Ptolemy, the Macedonian, son of Glaucias, to the sub-administrator Sarapion, for the delivery of arrears of their allowance of oil to two twin sisters attached to the service of the Temple of Serapis at Memphis, in Egypt; written in cursive uncial letters on papyrus. B.C. 162. [*Papyrus* xxi.]
2. HOMER'S ILIAD. Book xviii., lines 1–171. Found in a tomb, known as the Crocodile Pit, at Ma'abdey near Monfalat in Egypt, in 1849. Written in uncial characters, on papyrus, in the First Century before Christ. [*Papyrus* cvii.]
3. ORATION OF HYPERIDES against Demosthenes, respecting the treasure of Harpalus; fragments. The only extant MS. of the Oration. Found in a tomb at Gournou in the district of Western Thebes in Egypt, in 1847. Written in uncials on papyrus, in the 1st century B.C. [*Papyrus* cviii.]
4. HOMER'S ILIAD: a leaf from a *palimpsest* manuscript [in which the original text of Homer has been erased to give place to a theological treatise in Syriac, of the 9th cent.], containing Book xiv., lines 224–256. Belonged to the Convent of St. Mary Deipara in the Nitrian Desert in Egypt. Written in uncials, in the 6th century. Vellum. [*Add. MS.* 17,210.]
5. PSALTER: one of a number of fragments, containing portions of Psalms 23, 24. Found among the rubbish of an ancient Convent at Thebes in Egypt, in 1836. Written in mixed capitals and uncials on papyrus in the 6th or 7th century. [*Papyrus* xxxvii.]
6. HYMNS used in the services of the Greek Church: fragments. Written in sloping uncials, in the 8th century. Vellum. [*Add. MS.* 26,113.]
7. GREEK-LATIN GLOSSARY. Written in uncials in the 7th

century, in the West of Europe, being copied from a mutilated original. Vellum. [*Harley MS.* 5792.]

8. The Four Gospels. Written in finely-formed uncials in the 9th or 10th century. Vellum. [*Add. MS.* 11,300.]
9. Byzantine Chronicles, of Nicephorus, Patriarch of Constantinople [806–815, d. 828], *etc.* Written in minuscules, late in the 9th century. Vellum. [*Add. MS.* 19,390.]
10. Evangeliarium, or lessons from the Gospels for services throughout the year. Written in sloping uncials of Sclavonic type, in the 9th or 10th century. Vellum. [*Harl. MS.* 5787.]
11. Scala Paradisi, by St. John Climacus, Abbat of Mount Sinai. Written in minuscules, in the 10th century. Vellum. [*Add. MS.* 17,471.]
12. Works of Lucian of Samosata. Written in fine minuscules, in the 10th century. Vellum. [*Harley MS.* 5694.]
13. Thucydides; with the commentary of Marcellinus. Written in minuscules in the 11th century. Vellum. [*Add. MS.* 11,727.]
14. The Four Gospels. Written in minuscules by the priest Synesius, in December, 1033. Vellum. [*Add. MS.* 17,470.]
15. Psalter, and Canticles; illustrated with paintings in the margins. Written in minuscules by Theodorus of Cæsarea, arch-priest, a.d. 1066. Vellum. [*Add. MS.* 19,352.]
16. Homer's Odyssey, with scholia. Written in minuscules, in the 13th century. Vellum. [*Harley MS.* 5674.]
17. Psalter, in *Greek*, *Latin*, and *Arabic*, in parallel columns. Written in minuscules, before a.d. 1153. Vellum. [*Harley MS.* 5786.]
18. Commentary on the Psalms, by Euthymius Zigabenus. Written in minuscules, by the monk Maximus, in July, 1281. Paper. [*Harley MS.* 5575.]
19. Treatises of St. Athanasius, Archbishop of Alexandria. Written in minuscules, much contracted, by Romanus the Reader, a.d. 1321. Paper. [*Harley MS.* 5579.]
20. Lexicon of Suidas. Written in minuscules, by Georgius Bœophorus, a.d. 1402. Paper. [*Add. MS.* 11,892.]
21. Homer's Iliad. Written in minuscules by a scribe

named Christopher, in Italy, A.D. 1431. Vellum. [*King's MS.* 16.]

22. HOMER'S ODYSSEY. Written in minuscules, by the priest Johannes Rhosus, of Crete, A.D. 1479. Vellum. [*Harley MS.* 5658.]

II.—LATIN AND OTHER MSS.

Case B.

23. THE FOUR GOSPELS in the *Latin* vulgate version. Written in uncials, probably in Italy, in the 6th or 7th century. Vellum. [*Harley MS.* 1775.]
24. HISTORY of PAULUS OROSIUS; fragments. *Latin.* Taken from the linings of the covers of a volume in the library of St. Remacle at Stabloo, or Stavelot, in Belgium. Written in uncials, late in the 7th century. Vellum. [*Add. MS.* 24,144.]
25. THEOLOGICAL TRACTS; with a Life of St. Furseus. *Latin.* Written in France, in uncials and minuscules, in the 7th and 9th centuries. Vellum. [*Harley MS.* 5041.]
26. ORIGEN'S Homilies on the Book of Numbers, in the *Latin* version of Rufinus. Belonged to the Abbey of Corbie, in France. Written in uncials, late in the 7th century. Vellum. [*Burney MS.* 340.]
27. THE FOUR GOSPELS, in the *Latin* vulgate version. Written in uncials for Abbat Atto, apparently of the monastery of St. Vincent, on the river Volturno, in the territory of Benevento in Italy, between A.D. 739 and 760. Vellum. [*Add. MS.* 5463.]
28. BEDE'S Ecclesiastical History. *Latin.* Partially injured by fire in 1731. Written in England, in pointed minuscules, in the 8th century. Vellum. [*Cotton MS.* Tiberius C. ii.]
29. THE FOUR GOSPELS, in the *Latin* vulgate version. Written in England, in half-uncials, in the 8th century. Vellum. [*Royal MS.* 1 B. vii.]
30. THE FOUR GOSPELS, in the *Latin* vulgate version. From the monastery of St. Augustine at Canterbury. Written in half-uncials of English type, late in the 8th century. Vellum. [*Royal MS.* 1 E. vi.]

31. Liber Vitæ, or lists of the names of benefactors of the church of St. Cuthbert at Lindisfarne, afterwards removed to Durham; together with the names of those who were entitled to the prayers of the monks by the ties of confraternity, *etc.* *Latin.* Written in half-uncials, in gold and silver, about A.D. 840. Vellum. [*Cotton MS.* Domitian A. vii.]
32. Lessons and Prayers. *Latin.* Formerly belonged to Winchester. Written in round minuscules, in England, in the 8th century. Vellum. [*Harley MS.* 2965.]
33. Lessons, Prayers, and Hymns. *Latin.* Written in round minuscules, in England, in the 8th century. Vellum. [*Royal MS.* 2 A. xx.]
34. Litany and Prayers. *Latin.* Written in round minuscules, probably in Ireland, in the 8th or 9th century. Vellum. [*Harley MS.* 7653.]
35. Treatises of St. Jerome, and St. Cyprian; with tracts on the paschal cycle, *etc.* Written in minuscules, in England, in the 9th century. Vellum. [*Cotton MS.* Caligula A. xv.]
36. Commentary of Theodore, Bishop of Mopsuestia, on the Pauline Epistles. *Latin.* Written in Italy, in Lombardic minuscules, in the 9th century. Vellum. [*Harley MS.* 3063.]
37. St. Gregory's "Moralia," or commentary on the Book of Job. *Latin.* Written in France, in Merovingian mintuscules, in the 7th century. Vellum. [*Add. MS.* 11,878.]
38. St. Gregory's "Moralia," or commentary on the Book of Job. *Latin.* Written in France, in Merovingian minuscules, in the 8th century. Vellum. [*Add. MS.* 31,031.]
39. Theological Tracts and excerpts. *Latin.* Written in minuscules, apparently in France, in the 8th century. Vellum. [*Cotton MS.* Nero A. ii.]
40. Orationale Gothicum: containing prayers for the services in the early Mozarabic Liturgy. *Latin.* From the monastery of S. Domingo de Silos, near Burgos, in Spain. Written in Visigothic minuscules, in Spain, in the 9th century. Vellum. [*Add. MS.* 30,852.]
41. Lives and Passions of Saints; with large ornamental initials. *Latin.* Written, in Visigothic minuscules, by the deacon Gomes, at the order of Damian, abbat of the

monastery of S. Pedro de Cardeña, in the diocese of Burgos, in Spain, A.D. 919. Vellum. [*Add. MS.* 25,600.]

42. THE FOUR GOSPELS, in the *Latin* vulgate version. From the monastery of St. Geneviève in Paris. Written in gold Caroline minuscules, in the latter part of the 9th century. Vellum. [*Harley MS.* 2797.]

43. THE FOUR GOSPELS, in the *Latin* vulgate version. From the monastery of Eller, near Cochem, on the Mosel. Written in small Caroline minuscules, in the 9th or 10th century. Vellum. [*Harley MS.* 2826.]

44. THE FOUR GOSPELS, in the *Latin* vulgate version. Written in Caroline minuscules, in red ink, in the 9th or 10th century. [*Harley MS.* 2795.]

45. THE FOUR GOSPELS, in the *Latin* vulgate version; with ornamental initials and borders. Written in Caroline minuscules in the 9th or 10th century. Vellum. [*Add. MS.* 11,849.]

46. THE FOUR GOSPELS, in the *Latin* vulgate version. From St. Petroc's Priory at Bodmin, in Cornwall. Written in Caroline minuscules, early in the 10th century. On the margins and blank leaves were entered, from time to time, records of the manumission of serfs publicly made at the altar of St. Petroc. Vellum. [*Add. MS.* 9381.]

47. THE BIBLE, according to the *Latin* vulgate version of St. Jerome, revised by Theodulph, Bishop of Orleans. From the monastery of St. Hubert, in the diocese of Liége. Written in a very small minuscule hand, in triple columns, in the 9th century. Vellum. [*Add. MS.* 24,142.]

48. THE FOUR GOSPELS, in the *Latin* vulgate version. From the abbey of St. Martin of Tours. Written in Caroline minuscules, late in the 9th century. Vellum. [*Egerton MS.* 609.]

49. PSALTER, in Tironian Notes, the shorthand characters invented by Marcus Tullius Tiro, the freedman of Cicero. *Latin.* From the abbey of St. Rémy, at Rheims. Written early in the 10th century. Vellum. [*Add. MS.* 9046.]

50. LEXICON TIRONIANUM: or explanations of the Tironian Notes, the shorthand characters invented by Marcus Tullius Tiro, freedman of Cicero. *Latin.*

Written, probably in France, early in the 10th century. Vellum. [*Add. MS.* 21,164.]

51. CICERO's "Aratea": with drawings of the constellations filled in with explanations of the figures taken from the "Poeticon Astronomicon" of Hyginus. Written in Caroline minuscules, the extracts from Hyginus being in rustic capitals, in the 9th or 10th century. Vellum. [*Harley MS.* 647.]

52. VITRUVIUS "de Architectura." From the abbey of St. Pantaleon at Cologne. Written in Caroline minuscules, late in the 9th century. Vellum. [*Harley MS.* 2767.]

53. JUVENAL's Satires. Written in Caroline minuscules, early in the 10th century. Vellum. [*Add. MS.* 15,600.]

54. HORACE's works; with glosses and scholia. Written in Caroline minuscules, early in the 10th century. Vellum. [*Harley MS.* 2725.]

55. THE BIBLE, in the *Latin* vulgate version; with miniatures and initials. Written for the monastery of St. Mary de Parco, near Louvain, A.D. 1148. Vellum. [*Add. MS.* 14,790.]

56. ORIGEN's Homilies in the *Latin* version of Rufinus and Jerome; with coloured initials. Written in the monastery of St. Mary at Cambron, in the diocese of Cambray, Belgium, A.D. 1163. Vellum. [*Add. MS.* 15,307.]

57. THE BIBLE, in the *Latin* vulgate version; with miniatures and illuminated initials. Written for the abbey of Floreffe near Namur, in Belgium, about A.D. 1160. Vellum. [*Add. MS.* 17,738.]

58. THE BIBLE, in the *Latin* vulgate version; with illuminated initials. Written in France, in the 13th century. Vellum. [*Add. MS.* 15,253.]

59. CÆSAR's Commentaries "de bello Gallico." Written in France, in the 11th century. Vellum. [*Add. MS.* 10,084.]

60. CICERO "De oratore." Written in France, in the 10th century. Vellum. [*Harley MS.* 2736.]

61. THE BOOK OF LEVITICUS and the Gospel of St. John, with commentary and glosses. Written in the Abbey of St. Mary of Buildwas, in Shropshire, A.D. 1176 Vellum. [*Harley MS.* 3038.]

62. RULE of St. Benedict. *Latin.* Written in the monastery of St. Gilles, in the diocese of Nîmes, in the South of France, A.D. 1129. Vellum. [*Add. MS.* 16,979.]

63. THE BIBLE, in the *Latin* vulgate version. Written probably in Northern France, in the 11th century. Vellum. [*Royal MS.* 1 E. viii.]

64. HOMILIES of St. Ambrose, St. Gregory, *etc.*, and lessons from the Gospels and Epistles; with coloured initials. *Latin.* Written in Italy, early in the 12th century. Vellum. [*Harley MS.* 7183.]

65. THE BIBLE, in the *Latin* vulgate version; with illuminated initials. From the monastery of St. Mary at Worms, in Germany. Written in the 12th century. Vellum. [*Harley MS.* 2803.]

66. GRADUAL, or musical services for the Mass; with illuminated initials. *Latin.* Written in Italy, about A.D. 1400. Vellum. [*Add. MS.* 18,161.]

67. GRATIAN'S "Decretorum discordantium Concordia;" with commentary. With miniatures and illuminated initials. Written in Italy in the 14th century. Vellum. [*Add. MS.* 15,274.]

68. THE BIBLE, in the *Latin* vulgate version; with miniatures and illuminated initials and borders. Written in England, early in the 15th century. Vellum. [*Royal MS.* 1 E. ix.]

69. EARLY ENGLISH Poems and prose treatises; with illuminated initials and borders. Written about A.D. 1380–1400. Vellum. [*Add. MS.* 22,283.]

70. "CHRONIQUES D'ANGLETERRE": chronicle of the history of England, by Jehan de Wavrin; the third volume containing the history of the years 1377–1387. With illustrations and illuminated initials and borders. Written and illuminated for the use of King Edward IV., probably at Bruges, in Belgium, about the year 1480. Vellum. [*Royal MS.* 14 E. iv.]

71. "CHRONIQUES DE ST. DENYS": chronicle of the history of France, carried down to A.D. 1461. With illustrations and illuminated initials and borders. Written in the latter part of the 15th century. Vellum. [*Royal MS.* 20 E. 1.]

72. ST. AUGUSTINE'S Commentary on the Psalms; with illuminated initials and borders. *Latin.* Written in

Italy for Ferdinand of Aragon, King of Naples, A.D. 1480. Vellum. [*Add. MS.* 14,779.]

Case C.

73. Mariale: hymns to the Virgin, Penitential Psalms, *etc.* *Latin.* Written in England or Northern France, early in the 13th century. Vellum. [*Cotton MS.* Titus A. xxi.]
74. Missal, of the use of the Church of St. Bavon of Ghent; with musical notation. *Latin.* With illuminated initials. Written at the end of the 12th century. Vellum. [*Add. MS.* 16,949.]
75. Breviary, of English use. *Latin.* Written, probably at St. Albans, late in the 12th century. Vellum. [*Royal MS.* 2 A. xx.]
76. The Four Gospels; in the *Latin* vulgate version; with coloured initials, of interlaced designs. Written by Mælbrigte Hua Maluanaigh, at Armagh, in Ireland, A.D. 1138. Vellum. [*Harley MS.* 1802.]
77. The Bible, in the *Latin* vulgate version; with illuminated initials. Written, probably in England, in the 13th century. Vellum. [*Add. MS.* 15,452.]
78. Herbal, compiled from Dioscorides, *etc.*; with coloured illustrations of plants. *Latin.* Written in England early in the 13th century. Vellum. [*Sloane MS.* 1975.]
79. Liber de natura Bestiarum: a treatise on the nature of beasts, birds and fishes, with coloured illustrations. Written in England early in the 13th century. Vellum. [*Harley MS.* 3244.]
80. Missal, of the use of Amiens; with musical notation. *Latin.* Written in France, A.D. 1218. Vellum. [*Add. MS.* 17,742.]
81. Martyrology, founded on Usuardus, *etc.* *Latin.* Probably belonged to the Church of St. Bartholomew at Benevento. Written in Italy, in Lombardic minuscules, in the 13th century. [*Add. MS.* 23,776.]
82. The Bible, in the *Latin* vulgate version, with marginal commentary. With illuminated initials. Written in France, in the 13th century. [*Harley MS.* 404.]
83. Psalter, with illuminated initials and borders. *Latin.* Written in England, early in the 14th century. Vellum. [*Lansdowne MS.* 346.]

84. LAWS of ALFONSO X., King of Castile and Leon [A.D. 1252–1284], known as "Las Partidas"; with small miniatures. *Spanish.* Written at the beginning of the 14th century. Vellum. [*Add. MS.* 20,787.]

85. "LE LIVRE DOU TRESOR": an encyclopædic treatise, by Brunetto Latini; with illuminated initials. *French.* Written in the 14th century. Vellum. [*Add. MS.* 30,025.]

86. PSALTER, Litany, etc.: with illuminated initials and borders. *Latin.* Belonged to Philippa of Hainault [d. 1369], Queen of Edward III. Written in England, in the 14th century. Vellum. [*Harley MS.* 2899.]

87. THE BLACK BOOK of the Admiralty, with illuminated initials and borders. *French* and *Latin.* Written in England, early in the 15th century. Vellum. [*Cotton MS.* Vespasian B. xxii.]

88. MEDICAL Treatises, by John Arderne and others; with marginal illustrations. *Latin* and *English.* Written in England, early in the 15th century. Vellum. [*Add. MS.* 29,301.]

89. SELECT PSALMS; with illuminated initials and borders. *Latin.* Written in England for Humphrey, Duke of Gloucester, brother of Henry V. [d. 1446], in the 15th century. Vellum. [*Royal MS.* 2 B. i.]

90. LUCAN'S "Pharsalia"; with illuminated initials. Written at Ferrara in Italy by "Jacobus Juliani de Portiolo" for Feltrino Boiardo, of Reggio, A.D. 1378. Vellum. [*Add. MS.* 11,990.]

91. VALERIUS MAXIMUS "de Romanorum exterorumque factis et dictis memorabilibus"; with coloured initials. Written in Italy by "Filipinus de Gandinonibus," A.D. 1412; and sold by him to Bertolino de' Medici on 22 Oct. 1440, for 10 ducats. Vellum. [*Add. MS.* 14,095.]

92. LUCRETIUS "de Rerum Natura"; with illuminated initials. Written in Italy by "Joannes Rainaldus Mennius" in the 15th century. Vellum. [*Add. MS.* 11,912.]

93. POEM in praise of, and dedicated to, Lodovico Maria Sforza Visconti, Duke of Bari, who succeeded as Duke of Milan in A.D. 1494; by Bernardino de' Capitanei da Landriano. *Italian.* With illuminated border and initials. About A.D. 1480–1490. Vellum. [*Add. MS.* 14,817.]

94. St. Gregory's Dialogues; with illuminated initials. *Spanish.* Written in the middle of the 15th century. Vellum. [*Add. MS.* 30,039.]
95. St. Jerome's Epistles, etc.; with miniatures and borders. *Latin.* Written in France, in the Italian style, late in the 15th century. Vellum. [*Add. MS.* 30,051.]
96. Offices of the Virgin; with illuminated initials. *Latin.* Written in France, late in the 15th century. Vellum. [*Sloane MS.* 3981.]

III.—ENGLISH MSS.

Case D.

97. Beowulf: Epic poem in *Anglo-Saxon.* The unique manuscript. Written in England, about A.D. 1000. Vellum. [*Cotton MS.* Vitellius A. xv.]
98. The Anglo-Saxon Chronicle, from the Invasion of Julius Cæsar to A.D. 1066. Written in the same hand to A.D. 1046, and afterwards in various hands. Vellum. [*Cotton MS.* Tiberius B. i.]
99. The Creed, Lord's Prayer, *etc.*, followed by a Bestiary, in English verse; with other pieces, in *Latin*, *English*, and *French.* Written in England, in the 13th century. Vellum. [*Arundel MS.* 292.]
100. Lives of St. Katharine, St. Margaret, and St. Julian, with verses on the Passion of Christ, etc.; in *English.* Written in the first half of the 13th century. Vellum. [*Royal MS.* 17 A. xxvii.]
101. The "Ancren Rewle," Homilies, Lives of Saints, etc.; in *English.* Written in the first half of the 13th century. Vellum. [*Cotton MS.* Titus D. xviii.]
102. The "Aȝenbyte of Inwyt" (i. e. Remorse of Conscience), by Dan Michel of Northgate, in Kent, a monk of St. Augustine's Abbey, Canterbury. The author's autograph manuscript, written A.D. 1340. Vellum. [*Arundel MS.* 57.]
103. "Piers Plowman": a poem by William Langland, in *English* alliterative verse. Written before A.D. 1400. Vellum. [*Cotton MS.* Vespasian B. xvi.]

104. THE LAY FOLKS' MASS-BOOK, or manner of hearing Mass: in verse. A translation, made at the end of the 13th century, probably from the French, the original author being one "Dan Jeremy" [Jeremiah, Canon of Rouen and archdeacon of Cleveland, dioc. York, 1170–1175]. Late 14th century. Vellum. [*Royal MS.* 17 B. xvii.]

105. THE BIBLE, in the earlier Wycliffite version. Late 14th century. Vellum. [*Add. MS.* 15,580.]

106. THE NEW TESTAMENT, in the later Wycliffite version; with illuminated initials. First half of the 15th century. Vellum. [*Egerton MS.* 1171.]

107. THE CATHOLIC EPISTLES and Apocalypse, in the later Wycliffite version. First half of the 15th century. Vellum. [*Harley MS.* 5768.]

108. PSALTER, with Canticles, *etc.*, in *Latin* and *English*, verse by verse; the English version attributed to William de Schorham [Shoreham], who was admitted vicar of Chart Sutton, near Leeds, co. Kent, A.D. 1320. Written in the middle of the 14th century. Vellum. [*Add. MS.* 17,376.]

109. THE PRYMER, or Book of prayers, in *English*, containing the Hours of the Virgin, the dirge, penitential and other psalms, litany, etc.; with illuminated initials and borders. Early 15th century. Vellum. [*Add. MS.* 17,010.]

110. TRACTS "of wedded men and wyves," and on the Lord's Prayer, attributed to Wycliffe; with other pieces. First half of the 15th century. Vellum. [*Harley MS.* 2398.]

111. COMMENTARY on the Ten Commandments, attributed to Wycliffe; with other tracts. Middle of the 15th century. Vellum. [*Royal MS.* 17 A. xxvi.]

112. CHAUCER'S "Canterbury Tales." Early 15th century. Vellum. [*Lansdowne MS.* 851.]

113. CHAUCER'S "Troilus and Cressida." Early 15th century. Vellum. [*Harley MS.* 2280.]

114. GOWER'S "Confessio Amantis." Early 15th century. Vellum. [*Add. MS.* 12,043.]

115. THOMAS OCCLEVE'S poem, "De regimine Principum." With portrait of Geoffrey Chaucer. Early 15th century. Vellum. [*Harley MS.* 4866.]

116. JOHN LYDGATE'S poem, "The Storie of Thebes";

followed by Occleve's "De regimine Principum." Middle of the 15th century. Vellum. [*Add. MS.* 18,632.]

117. JOHN CAPGRAVE's poem on the Life of St. Katherine. 15th century. Belonged to Campsey Priory, co. Suffolk, by the gift of Dame Katherine Babyngton, sub-prioress. Vellum. [*Arundel MS.* 396.]

118. MYSTERY-PLAYS, on subjects taken from the Old and New Testaments; said to have been represented at Coventry on the Feast of Corpus Christi. Written in 1468. Paper. [*Cotton MS.* Vespasian D. viii.]

119. CHRONICLE of ENGLAND, known as "The Brut," ending with the siege of Rouen in A.D. 1418–9. 15th century. Vellum. [*Harley MS.* 24.]

120. METRICAL CHRONICLE of England to A.D. 1271, attributed to Robert of Gloucester. 15th cent. Vellum. [*Harley MS.* 201.]

121. TRAVELS of Sir John Mandeville: *English* version. 15th century. [*Add. MS.* Titus C. xvi.]

IV.—ORIENTAL MSS.

Case E.

122. The Books of the former and latter Prophets, viz., Joshua, Judges, Samuel, Kings, Isaiah, Jeremiah, and Ezekiel, provided with vowel-points and accents, and accompanied by the Masora Magna and Parva. One of the earliest *Hebrew* Biblical MSS. Written in a Spanish hand of the 12th cent. Vellum. [*Harley MS.* 5720.]

123. The Recognitions of Clement of Rome; the discourses of Titus, Bishop of Bostra, against the Manichæans; the treatise of Eusebius of Cæsarea on the Theophania; and other works. *Syriac.* Written at Edessa, A.D. 411. Vellum. The oldest *dated* volume extant. [*Add. MS.* 12,150.]

124. The Samaritan Pentateuch. *Hebrew;* A.D. 1356. The earliest *dated* Samaritan MS. in the Department. Paper. [*Oriental MS.* 2683.]

125. The Machbereth, or *Hebrew* Lexicon, of Menachem ben Sārūk, and other works. A.D. 1091. The earliest

dated Hebrew MS. in the Department. Vellum. [*Add. MS.* 27,214.]

126. The History of King Lālībalā of Lāsta, surnamed Gabra Maskal, or "Servant of the Cross." *Ethiopic.* Written between A.D. 1400 and 1434. The oldest MS. in the collection taken at Magdala, in 1868. Vellum. [*Oriental MS.* 719.]

127. The Coran. *Arabic;* written in the Maghribi or Western character, about A.D. 1200. Vellum. [*Oriental MS.* 1270.]

128. *Kitāb al Ghādī wa 'l-Mughtadī:* a treatise on the nourishment of the various parts of the human body, by Ibn Abi 'l-Ash'ath, an Arab physician of the 10th cent. *Arabic.* A.D. 960. The earliest *dated* Arabic MS. in the Department, and one of the earliest paper MSS. extant. [*Oriental MS.* 2600.]

129. The four Gospels, written in uncial letters, with illuminated initials and portraits of the Evangelists. *Armenian.* A.D. 1181. The earliest *dated* Armenian MS. in the Department. Vellum. [*Oriental MS.* 81.]

130. Fragments of the Gospels of St. Matthew and St. John, in *Syriac*, according to the Peshīttā version, with an *Arabic* translation, written in parallel columns. Early 10th century. Vellum. [*Add. MS.* 14,467.]

131. Fragment of the Coran (Surah XXXVII. v. 105–109) in the Cufic character, with a few vowels marked by red dots, and, in the case of various readings, by green dots, but without diacritical points. *Arabic.* Apparently of the 9th century. Vellum. [*Add. MS.* 11,362.]

132. Tarikh Yamini: a history of Sultan Mahmud Ghaznavi. *Persian.* A.H. 664; A.D. 1266. One of the earliest *dated* Persian MSS. [*Add.* 24,950.]

133. *Piste Sophia*, a gnostic work ascribed to Valentinus. *Coptic.* 7th cent. The earliest Coptic MS. in the Department. Vellum. [*Add. MS.* 5114.]

134. Fragment of the Coran (Surah V. v. 2–4, Surah VI. v. 39–44) in the Cufic character, with a few diacritical marks in the shape of thin oblique lines, but without any vowels. *Arabic.* Probably of the 8th century. Vellum. [*Add. MS.* 11,737.]

Case F.

135. A Pali manuscript in the Kambojian character, containing Buddhaghosha's Commentary on the *Paṭṭhānappakaraṇam*, the seventh book of the Abhidhammapiṭakam. Written on 147 leaves of the talipot palm-tree. [*Add. MS.* 11,552.] *Presented in* 1839, *by James Barlow Hoy, Esq.*

136. Envelope of an *Ola* or Letter addressed to the Governor of Ceylon, written in the Cingalese character on a leaf of the talipot, and ornamented with gold. It is accompanied by a gold tissue case worked with flowers. [*Sloane MS.* 3478.]

137. The *Bhagavad Gítá*, in Sanscrit, written on a long roll of thin paper, with miniatures; mounted on rollers, in a morocco box. [*Add. MS.* 4829.] *Presented by Alexander Dow, Esq., in* 1767.

138. The *Srí Bhagavat Purána*, in Sanscrit, very beautifully written and illuminated, on a roll of thin paper, above 65 feet in length; mounted on rollers, in a morocco case. [*Add. MS.* 16,624.]

139. The *Durgá-pátha*, a Sanscrit poem, in praise of the goddess Durga, written in very minute characters, on a small roll of thin paper, with miniatures; mounted on rollers, in a morocco case. [*Add. MS.* 16,628.]

140. A work in the Javanese character, written on palm-leaves; and enclosed within carved wooden covers. [*Add. MS.* 12,276.]

141. A Tamul manuscript, on leaves of the talipot tree, bound in a frame of gilt copper, made in the form of a tortoise. [*Add. MS.* 6780.] *Presented in* 1828, *by Robert Ray, Esq.*

142. A manuscript in the Batta character, written on a long piece of bark, folded so as to resemble a book, and containing various magical directions, charms, &c. [*Add. MS.* 4726.] *Presented in* 1764, *by Alexander Hall, Esq.*

143. A manuscript written in the Kannadi language, on strips of the palm-leaf, rolled up into the form of rings. It contains memoranda of revenue accounts, under the Mysore government. [*Add. MS.* 12,092.]

144–146. Three small rolls written on the inner bark of the birch-tree, in very minute Sanscrit characters, containing the *Srí Bhagavad Gítá—One of these was purchased in* 1832; *the second was presented by the Rev. D. Warren, in* 1833; *and the third by Samuel Allen, Esq., in* 1843. [*Add. MSS.* 8892, 9287, 14,338.]

147. A small volume, containing the Sanscrit poem called *Durgá-pátha*, written in gold letters, on a purple ground, with miniatures. [*Add. MS.* 18,184.]

148. The *Siva Kavacha*, a poem in Sanscrit, written in silver letters on a black ground, with miniatures. [*Add. MS.* 16,627.]

149. A Pali manuscript in the Cingalese character, containing the *Satipaṭṭhāna Sutta*, a portion of the Buddhistic Canon. Written on 53 leaves of copper gilt. [*Add. MS.* 12,091.]

150. A Pali manuscript in the Cingalese character, containing the *Dhammacakkappavattana Sutta*, Buddha's first sermon preached at Benares, and the *Cūlakammavibhanga Sutta*. Beautifully engraved on 25 leaves of silver. [*Egerton MS.* 764.]

151. A Pali manuscript in the square Burmese character, containing part of the first chapter of the Buddhistic ritual, entitled *Kammavācam*. Written on three lacquered palm-leaves with inlaid mother-of-pearl letters. [*Add. MS.* 23,939.]

152. A Pali manuscript in the Burmese character, containing the first chapter of the *Kammavācam*. Written on five leaves of the talipot, on a gold ground. [*Add. MS.* 15,290.]

153. A thin plate of gold, inscribed on both sides in the Javanese character, being probably a letter from one of the native Princes. [*Egerton MS.* 765.]

154. A Pali manuscript in the Cingalese character, containing the *Visuddhi-maggo*, Buddhaghosha's compendium of the Buddhistic Canon. Written on 236 palm-leaves, and enclosed in carved ivory covers. [*Add. MS.* 11,658.]

155. A Pàli manuscript in the square Burmese character, containing the first three chapters of the *Kammavācam*. Written on twelve leaves of the talipot tree, on a lacquered gold ground. [*Add. MS.* 11,640.]

156. A Pali manuscript in the square Burmese character, containing the first two chapters of the *Kammavācam*. Written on fourteen leaves of ivory. [*Add. MS.* 15,291.]

157. A Cingalese stylus, or instrument of brass for writing

on palm-leaves, with the wooden case in which it is usually enclosed. [*Add. MS.* 11,556.] *Presented in* 1839, *by James Barlow Hoy, Esq.*

158. A large folio volume, containing a collection of fine Hindoo miniatures and portraits, with specimens of Persian penmanship by eminent caligraphists, between A.H. 1011–1152 (A.D. 1602–1739). [*Add. MS.* 21,928.]

159. A Buddhistic work, written in gold letters on an azure ground, in the ancient Chinese character, and illustrated with mythological paintings on the leaves of the *Ficus religiosa.* Explanations of these are inserted in the modern Chinese character. [*Add. MS.* 14,423.]

160. A Poem in Hindustani, by Mohammed Wájid Ali, ex-King of Oude, lithographed in imitation of a manuscript, at Lucknow, and ornamented with gold. Quarto. *Presented in* 1855, *by the King's Minister.* [*Add. MS.* 21,159.]

161. The Four Gospels, in Armenian, written on cotton paper, and ornamented with miniatures, of the 16th century. In the original stamped leather binding, with metal ornaments; and enclosed in a flowered satin case, embroidered with silver. [*Add. MS.* 7940.]

162. Hymns in praise of St. George and the Virgin, in the Ethiopic language, written on vellum, in the present century. In the native binding of wooden boards, enclosed in a leathern case. [*Add. MS.* 18,995.]

163. The Coran, written in minute Arabic characters, on a long roll of thin glazed paper; mounted on rollers, in a morocco case. [*Add. MS.* 5904.] *Presented by Thomas Park, Esq., in* 1804.

164. The Coran, in Arabic, written in the 19th century; enclosed in a green satin case, embroidered with the arms of the late Duke of Sussex, to whose collection it belonged. [*Add. MS.* 15,266.]

165. Mirkhond's General History, intitled *Rauzat-us-Safá;* written for the Sherif Haji Mir Husaina, A.H. 1258–61 (A.D. 1842–5). On the covers are paintings representing the battle of Karnal, A.D. 1739, and hunting scenes. [*Add. MS.* 18,540.]

166. An Oriental Album, containing numerous specimens of Persian and Arabic writing, with many miniatures, and portraits of historical personages, executed A.H. 965–1219 (A.D. 1558–1804). [*Add. MS.* 7468.]

167. *Yúsuf u Zulaikhá*, a Poem in Persian, by Firdausi,

written A.H. 1055 (A.D. 1645); a work of which only three other copies are known to exist; in a very beautiful modern Oriental binding. [*Add. MS.* 24,093.]

168. *Khizr Khán*, a Poem in Persian, by Amir Khusrau of Delhi, written in a beautiful Talik character, on gold-sprinkled paper, and ornamented with miniatures, apparently of the 16th century. [*Add. MS.* 7754.]

169. The *Díwán*, or Lyric Poems of the Persian Poet Háfiz; written on gold-sprinkled paper, apparently in the 17th century, with miniatures and borders. In the original binding. [*Add. MS.* 7763.]

EARLY BIBLICAL MSS.

[Exhibited in Cases G–K, against the pilasters.]

Case G.

1. A volume of the celebrated "CODEX ALEXANDRINUS," containing the *Greek* Text of the Holy Scriptures written in uncial letters on very thin vellum, probably in the middle of the 5th century. Presented to King Charles I. by Cyril, Patriarch of Constantinople. [*Royal MS.* 1 D. viii.]

2. The books of Genesis and Exodus, according to the *Peshito* or *Syriac* version; written at Amid, in Diarbekr, by a deacon named John, in the year 775 of the Seleucian era, A.D. 464, when Maras, the second of the name, was bishop of that city. Believed to be the earliest *dated* MS. extant of any entire books of the Scriptures. The volume also contains the books of Numbers and Deuteronomy, of about the same age, but written by a different hand. [*Add. MS.* 14,423.]

Case H.

The Bible, in *Latin*, of St. Jerome's version, as revised by Alcuin, Abbat of Tours, by command of the Emperor Charlemagne, between the years 796 and 800. The present copy was probably written about the year 840, and is adorned with large miniatures, and numerous initial letters in gold and silver. Vellum. [*Add. MS.* 10,546.]

In the Lower Division is shown a Bible, in *Latin*, of St. Jerome's version. Written by Goderannus and Ernestus, monks of the Abbey of St. Remacle at Stabloo or Stavelot, in Belgium, and illuminated and bound within four years ending in A.D. 1097. Vellum. [*Add. MS.* 28,107.]

Case I.

The Bible in the earlier *English* version of Wycliffe, beginning with the Book of Proverbs; with illuminated initials and borders. Late 14th century. The MS. belonged to Thomas of Woodstock, Duke of Gloucester, youngest son of Edward III., who was put to death by his nephew, Richard II., in the year 1397. His shield of arms is introduced into the illuminated border of the first page. Vellum. [*Egerton MS.* 617.]

Case K.

A large double roll, containing the Pentateuch, written on brown African goatskins, 89 feet in length by 26 inches in width, in a fine square uniform character, without points or apices. Probably of the 14th century; mounted on rollers. [*Harley MS.* 7619.]

In the Lower Division are placed three other vellum rolls of the Hebrew Pentateuch, of the 14th and 15th centuries, mounted on rollers, and enclosed in damask silk capsules or covers. *One of these was presented by Solomon da Costa, Esq., in* 1759; *the others were purchased in* 1836 *and* 1841. [*Add. MSS.* 11,828, 11,829; *Egerton MS.* 610.]

HISTORICAL DEEDS AND PAPYRI.

[**Exhibited in frames fixed against the wainscot in the north-east and north-west corners of the room.**]

On the East Side.

A series of PAPYRI, four of which are written in *Coptic*, and one in *Greek*, relating to the Monastery of St.

Phœbammon, near Hermonthis in Egypt; of the 8th and 9th centuries. [*Papyri* lxxvi–lxxix, lxxxi.]

On the West Side.

1. Instrument written in *Latin*, on papyrus, 8½ feet in length by 1 foot in width, containing a deed of sale of a house and lands in the territory of Rimini; dated at Ravenna, 3 June, in the 7th year of the reign of Justin the Younger [A.D. 572]. From the Pinelli Library. [*Add. MS.* 5412.]
2. Passport, written on papyrus, and granted to a Copt by 'Abd al-Malik Ibn Yazid, Governor of Egypt, to proceed to al-Fustat (old Cairo); dated A.H. 133 (A.D. 750). [*Oriental MS.* 15.]
3. Photograph of the MAGNA CARTA of KING JOHN. Dated at Runnymede, 15 June, in the 17th year of his reign [A.D. 1215]. A fragment only of the Great Seal remains, and the document itself was so much damaged by the fire of 1731, as to be now almost illegible. The charter was given to Sir Robert Cotton, probably by Sir Edward Dering, in 1630, and is now in the Department. [*Cotton Ch.* xiii. 31.]
4. Autotype facsimile of a contemporary and official copy of the MAGNA CARTA, which was given to Sir Robert Cotton by Humphry Wyems in 1628, and is now in the Department. [*Cotton MS.* Augustus ii. 106.] A printed copy of the text is placed with it.*
5. Original Bull of POPE LEO X., conferring on King Henry VIII. the title of Defender of the Faith; dated at Rome, 5 id. [11] Oct., in the 9th year of his pontificate [A.D. 1521]. Signed by the Pope and many of the Cardinals. It was much damaged in the fire of 1731. [*Cotton MS.* Vit. B. xiv.]
6. Original Act, constituting a Municipal Council for the city of Cologne; and having appended the seals of the various Guilds. Dated 14 September, 1396. [*Add. Ch.* 13,946.] *Presented, in* 1858, *by Octavius Morgan, Esq., M.P.*

* Copies of the autotype and printed text are sold in the British Museum.

MISCELLANEOUS DOCUMENTS.

[On the south-east and north-east pilasters.]

1. WILLIAM SHAKSPEARE. Autotype facsimile of the original Mortgage Deed, by which "William Shakespeare, of Stratford upon Avon, Gentleman," and others, grant on lease to Henry Walker, citizen of London, a dwelling-house, within the precincts of "the late Black Fryers," for the term of 100 years, at a peppercorn rent; with a proviso for the determination of the lease on the 29th September following. Dated 11 March, 10 Jac. I. 1612 [1613]. Four labels with seals are attached, on the first of which is the signature "Wm. SHAKSPe." Attached to the first two labels are seals bearing the initials H. L., probably belonging to Henry Lawrence, servant to the scrivener who prepared the lease. The original is in the Department. [*Egerton MS.* 1787].*
2. EDMUND SPENSER. Grant from the Poet, Edmund Spenser, styled "of Kilcolman, Esq." to — McHenry (a member of the Roche family), of the custody of the woods of Balliganin, *etc.*, in the county of Cork, Ireland. Not dated. *Holograph.* [*Add. MS.* 19,869.]
3. JOHN MILTON. Original Articles of Agreement, dated 27 April, 1667, between John Milton, gentleman, and Samuel Symmons, printer, for the sale of the copyright of "a Poem intituled *Paradise Lost.*" Signed "JOHN MILTON," with his seal of arms affixed. [*Add. MS.* 18,861.] *Presented, in* 1852, *by Samuel Rogers, Esq.*
4. HORATIO, VISCOUNT NELSON. Sketch-plan of the Battle of Aboukir, also called the Battle of the Nile. In the corner is the following attestation:—"This was drawn by Lord Viscount Nelson's left hand, the only remaining one, in my presence, this Friday, February 18th, 1803, at No. 23, Piccadilly, the house of Sir William Hamilton, late Ambassador at Naples, who was present. ALEXANDER STEPHENS." [*Add. MS.* 18,676.]
5. ARTHUR WELLESLEY, DUKE OF WELLINGTON. Enumeration, in his handwriting, of the cavalry under his command previous to the Battle of Waterloo, 18 June,

* Copies of this autotype are sold in the British Museum.

1815. [*Add. MS.* 7140.] *Presented, in* 1828, *by the Rt. Rev. John Jebb, D.D., Bishop of Limerick.*

6. (a.) General Charles George Gordon. Imperial Decree of the Emperor of China, conferring on General [then Major] Gordon, in command of "The Ever-victorious Army," an order of merit of the first rank, and a gift of 10,000 *taels* of silver, for his services in the capture of Soochow from the Tai Ping Rebels in 1863.

(b.) "Sketch Map of the districts [around Soochow] in possession of the [Tai Ping] Rebels in the years 1862, 63, 64; with dates of captures, &c. &c."; drawn by General Gordon.

Presented, in 1886, *by Sir Henry William Gordon, K.C.B.*

SEALS.

[Exhibited in the tables near the entrance to the King's Library.]

TABLE N.

Great Seals of the Sovereigns of England.

1\. 2. Edward the Confessor. Obverse and reverse of the 2nd seal. [1059–1066.]

3\. William I. Obverse of the 1st seal. [1075–1085.]

4\. William II. [1087–1100.] Sulphur cast of the reverse.

5\. Henry I. Obverse of the 4th seal. [1106–1135.]

6\. Stephen. Obverse of the 2nd seal. [1139–1144.]

7\. Henry II. [1154-1189.] Obverse of the 1st seal. No date.

8\. Richard I. Obverse of the 1st seal. 1190.

9\. Richard I. Obverse of the 2nd seal. 1197.

10\. John. [1199–1216.] Obverse of the only seal. No date.

11\. 12. Henry III. Obverse and reverse of the 1st seal. 1230, 1243.

13\. Henry III. Obverse of the 2nd seal. [About 1259.]

14\. 15. Edward I. Obverse and reverse of the only seal. 1276, 1285.

16\. 17. Edward II. Obverse and reverse of the only seal. 1323.

18. Edward III. Obverse of the 2nd seal. 1331.
19. Edward III. Obverse of the 3rd seal. 1338.
20. Edward III. Obverse of the 7th seal. [1340–1360.]
21. Edward III. Obverse of the 8th, or "Bretigny" seal. [1366–1375.]
22. Richard II. [1377–1399.] Obverse of the 1st seal. No date.
23. Richard II. Obverse of the 2nd seal. No date.
24. Henry IV. [1399–1413.] Obverse of the 2nd seal. Apparently from a deed dated 1408.
25. 26. Henry V. Obverse and reverse of the 1st seal. 1415.
27. Henry VI. Obverse of the 1st seal. 1442.
28. 29. Edward IV. Obverse and reverse of the 1st seal. [1461–1471.] 1462.
30. 31. Edward IV. Obverse and reverse of the 4th seal. [1471–1483.] 1471.
32. Richard III. Obverse of the only seal. 1484.
33. 34. Henry VII. Obverse and reverse of the only seal. 1507, 1486.
35. Henry VIII. Obverse of the 2nd seal. 1536. (The last great seal of England exhibiting gothic architecture.)
36. Henry VIII. Obverse of the 3rd seal. 1544.
37. 38. Edward VI. Obverse and reverse of the only seal. 1548, 1553.
39. 40. Mary I. Obverse and reverse of the only seal. No date, and 1554.
41. Philip I. and Mary I. [1554–1558.] Bronze cast of the obverse of the only seal.
42. 43. Elizabeth. Obverse and reverse of the first seal. No date [between 1558 and 1585], and 1559.
44. 45. Elizabeth. Obverse and reverse of the 2nd seal. No date [between 1585 and 1603], and 1598.
46. James I. [1603–1625.] Obverse of the 1st seal.
47. James I. Obverse of the 2nd seal.
48. 49. Charles I. Obverse and reverse of the 2nd seal. 1634, 1627.
50. 51. Commonwealth. Obverse in wax and reverse in sulphur of "the great seal of England. 1651." Used in 1656.
52. Republic. Reverse of the seal used during the Protectorate of Oliver Cromwell. [1658.]

53. Republic. [1658–1660.] Reverse of the seal used during the Protectorate of Richard Cromwell.
54. Charles II. [1649–1685.] Reverse of the 3rd seal. [Between 1661 and 1685.]
55. 56. Charles II. Obverse and reverse of the seal for Ireland. Dated "1660."
57. James II. Reverse of the only seal. 1686.
58. William III. and Mary II. [1689–1694.] Original design on stone for the reverse of a great seal.
59. William III. and Mary II. Reverse of the only seal. 1689.
60. Anne. Reverse of the 1st seal. 1704.
61. Anne. Sulphur cast of the obverse of the 2nd seal. [Matrix made in 1707.]
62. 63. George I. Obverse and reverse of the only seal. 1720; no date.
64. 65. George II. Obverse and reverse of the only seal. No date; 1748.
66. George III. [1760–1820.] Obverse of the 2nd seal. No date.
67. George III. Obverse of the 4th seal. No date.
68. George IV. Obverse of the only seal. [1824.]
69. 70. William IV. [1830–1837.] Proof impressions of the obverse and reverse of the only seal.
71. 72. Victoria. Proof impressions of the obverse and reverse of the 1st seal. [1837.]

TABLE O.

a.

Seals of Ecclesiastical Dignitaries.

1. Anselm, Archbishop of Canterbury. [1093–1107.]
2. Alexander, Bishop of Lincoln. 1145.
3. Theobald, Archbishop of Canterbury. [About 1144.]
4. Robert de Chesney or de Querceto, Bishop of Lincoln. 1152.
5. Richard Fitz-Neale, Bishop of London. [1189–1198.]
6. Geoffrey Plantagenet, Bishop of Lincoln. [1173–1181.]
7. William de Salso Marisco, Bishop of Llandaff. 1190.
8. Hugh, Bishop of Lincoln, 2nd seal. [1191–1195.]
9. Hubert, Archbishop of Canterbury. 1198.

10. Henry, Prior of Abergavenny, Bishop of Llandaff. [1193–1218.]
11. William of Blois, Bishop of Lincoln. [1203–1206.]
12. Stephen Langton, Archbishop of Canterbury. 1226.
13. Elias de Radnor, Bishop of Llandaff. [1230–1240.]
14. Chapter of Llandaff. [1230–1240.]
15. Walter de Suthfield, Bishop of Norwich. [1243–1257.]
16. Henry Lexington, Bishop of Lincoln. [1253–1258.]
17. Hugh Balsam, Bishop of Ely. 1266.
18. Lawrence de Sancto Martino, Bishop of Rochester. 1268.
19. William de Middleton, Bishop of Norwich. [1278–1288.]
20. William Fraser, Bishop of St. Andrews. 1281.
21. William de Luda, Archdeacon of Durham. 1286.
22. Anthony de Bek, Bishop of Durham. 1286.
23. John Le Romayne, Archbishop of York. 1293.
24. John Salmon, Bishop of Norwich. [1299–1325.]
25. John de Aldreby, Bishop of Lincoln. 1305.
26. Robert Winchelsey, Archbishop of Canterbury. 1309.
27. Richard de Kellawe, Bishop of Durham. [1311–1316.]
28. John de Eglescliffe, Bishop of Llandaff. [1323–1346.]
29. William de Melton, Archbishop of York. 1328.
30. Stephen de Gravesend, Bishop of London. 1337.
31. Ralph de Stratford, Bishop of London. 1340.
32. William Bateman, Bishop of Norwich. [1344–1355.]
33. John de Thoresby, Archbishop of York. [1353–1373.]
34. Simon de Sudbury, Archbishop of Canterbury. [1380–1381.] Seal "ad causas."
35. William Courtney, Archbishop of Canterbury. [1381–1396.]
36. John Bokyngham, Bishop of Lincoln. 1386.
37. Chapter of Lincoln. 1386.
38. Henry de Spencer, Bishop of Norwich. 1392.
39. Henry Beaufort, Bishop of Lincoln. 1403.
40. Richard Clifford, Bishop of London. 1409.
41. Philip de Repingdon, Bishop of Lincoln. 1415.
42. John Stafford, Archbishop of Canterbury. [1443–1452.] Seal "ad causas."
43. Richard Beauchamp, Bishop of Salisbury. 1470.
44. William Smith, Bishop of Lincoln. 1496.
45. William Wareham, Archbishop of Canterbury. [1504–1532.] Seal of Prerogative Court.

46. Thomas Cranmer, Archbishop of Canterbury. 1540.
47. Edward Lee, Archbishop of York. 1540.
48. Thomas Thirleby, Bishop of Westminster. (Design on wood.) [1540–1550.]
49. Nathaniel, Lord Crew, Bishop of Durham. [1674–1722.] Reverse of the "Palatine seal."

b.

SEALS OF ABBATS, ABBEYS, ETC.

1. Wilton, co. Wilts. [1372.] [The matrix being as early as the 11th cent.]
2. St. Mary's, York. [11th cent.]
3. Westacre, co. Norf. [About 1231–1236.] [11th cent. matrix.]
4. Selby, co. York. 1282. [12th cent. matrix.]
5. 6. Prior (Peter) and Priory of St. Peter's, Bath. [1159–1175.] [Matrix of the 10th or 11th cent.]
7. Newstead, co. Notts. [13th cent.]
8. Thornholm, co. Linc. 1297.
9. Nun Appleton, co. York. 1272.
10. William, Abbat of Lesnes, co. Kent. [12th cent.]
11. St. Alban's, co. Hertf. 1435. [12th cent. matrix.]
12. Daventre, co. Northt. 1295.
13. Nun Kelynge, co. York. [15th cent. charter, matrix 12th cent.]
14. Ankerwyke, co. Bucks. [13th cent.]
15. St. John of Leigh, co. Essex. [12th cent.]
16. St. Bartholomew, London. 1533. [13th cent. matrix.]
17. Kilburn, co. Midd. 1402. [13th cent. matrix.]
18. Battle, co. Suss. [13th cent.]
19. Greenfield, co. Linc. [About 1260.]
20. Peterborough, co. Northt. [13th cent.]
21. Oseney, co. Oxf. 1302.
22. St. James, Northampton. [About 1270.]
23. John, Abbat of St. Alban's. 1258.
24. Simon, Abbat of St. Edmund's Bury, co. Suff. [1257–1259.]
25. John de Medmeham, Abbat of Chertsey. [1268–1269.]
26. Chertsey, co. Surr. [1268–1269.]

27. Selborne, co. Hants. 1266.
28. Simon, Abbat of Kirkstede, co. Linc. [About 1278.]
29. Evesham, co. Worc. [13th cent.]
30. Hagneby, co. Linc. 1392. [13th cent. matrix.]
31. Barlings or Oxeney, co. Linc. 1310.
32. St. John's Redcliff, Bristol, co. Somers. [14th cent.] [Matrix older.]
33. Neuhus, co. Linc., 3rd seal. 1283.
34. Southwick, co. Hants. [13th cent.]
35. St. Oswald's, Bardney, co. Linc. 1347.
36. St. Paul's, London. [14th cent.]
37. Bridlington, co. York. 1327.
38. Merton, co. Surr. [14th cent.]
39. St. Edmund's Bury, co. Suff. 1518. [14th cent. matrix.]
40. John, Abbat of the above. 1518.
41. Boxgrove, co. Sussex. [14th cent.]
42. Bissemede, co. Bedf. 1523. [14th cent. matrix.]
43. St. Andrew's, Bromholme, co. Norf. 1421.
44. Holy Trinity, Norwich. 1321. [Matrix made in 1258.]
45. Christ Church, Canterbury. 1452.
46. Elsing Spittle, London. 1405.
47. Henry, Abbat of St. Werburg, Chester. 1394.
48. Waltham, co. Essex. 1537. [Matrix of different periods.]
49. Dean and Chapter of Ely, co. Cambr. [16th cent.]

c. d.

Baronial Seals.

1. Robert, Earl of Mellent. [11th cent.]
2. Hugh de Beauchamp. [11th cent.]
3. Ralph, son of Stephen de Oiland, or Hoiland. [11th cent.]
4. Milo de Gloecestria, 3rd Earl of Hereford. [1140–1143.]
5. Robert, son of Turketin, Knt. [1115–1150.]
6. Richard de Humet, King's Constable. [12th cent.]
7. Adam, son of Roger de Somerie. [13th cent.]
8. Roger de Mowbray, of co. York. [12th cent.]
9. Waleran de Bellomonte, Earl of Mellent. [Died 1166.]

10. Conan Le Petit, Duke of Brittany, 5th Earl of Richmond. [1165–1171.]
11. Geoffrey Plantagenet, son-in-law of the above, by some called 6th Earl of Richmond. [1168–1186.]
12. Simon de la Tour, Knt. [12th cent.]
13. Stephen de Thornham, Knt. [About 1194.]
14. Leisanus filius Morgani, of co. Glamorgan. [Early 13th cent.]
15. Gilbert Prudhomme. [Early 13th cent.]
16. Guillaume, Avoué of Arras, Lord of Béthune and Tenremonde. [13th cent.]
17. Briennus filius Radulphi, of co. Essex. [Early 13th cent.]
18. John, Earl of Moreton, afterwards King of England. [Before 1199.]
19. Alan, Count of Goelle, son of Stephen, Count of Ponthieu. 1202.
20. Baldwin, Count of Flanders. [Early 13th cent.]
21. Roger de Lacy, Constable of Chester. [1179–1213.]
22. Richard, Earl of Cornwall, younger son of King John. [1226–1272.]
23. The above, as King of the Romans. 1257.
24. Peter de Brus III. [13th cent.]
25. Robert, son of Walter de Davintre, of co. Northampton. [13th cent.]
26. Hugh de Neville. [1211–1223.]
27. Gilbert de Clare, Earl of Hertford. [1226–1313.]
28. John Fitz-Alan, of co. Warwick. [About 1272.]
29. Thomas de St. Walerie. [Early 13th cent.]
30. Helyas de Albeni. [Late 12th cent.]
31. Patrick Dunbar, 5th Earl of March. [1182–1232.]
32. Sir Robert de Ghisnes, Knt. [1242–1259.]
33. William de Fortibus, 7th Earl of Albemarle. [After 1251.]
34. Simon de Montfort, 2nd Earl of Leicester. 1258.
35. Geoffrey de Geynville of Ireland. 1259.
36. Patrick Dunbar, 9th Earl of March. [About 1260.]
37. Robert, son of William de Ferrers, Earl of Derby. 1262.
38. Peter de Montfort. [Middle of 13th cent.]
39. Roger de Quincy, 2nd Earl of Winchester. [1219–1264.]
40. John, Duke of Lorraine. 1295.

41. Sir John de la Hay, Knt. 1281.
42. Gerard de Furnivall. [Late 13th cent.]
43. Thomas, 2nd Earl of Lancaster. [1295–1321.]
44. John, Duke of Lorraine and Brabant. 1300.
45. Edmund Plantagenet, Earl of Cornwall. 1275.
46. Henry de Laci, 3rd Earl of Lincoln. 1331.
47. The same—a different seal. [About 1331.]
48. Theobald de Verdoun, Constable of Ireland. 1313.
49. William de Hoo, Knt. 1404.
50. John, son of Hubert de Burgh. [About 1269.]
51. John de Mowbray, Lord of the Island of Axholme [co. Linc.]. 1334.
52. William de Clinton, Earl of Huntingdon. 1366.
53. Hugh de Courtenay, 2nd Earl of Devon. 1349.
54. John Plantagenet "of Gaunt," Duke of Lancaster, Seneschal of England. (Privy seal.) 1363.
55. 56. Sir Robert de Marny, Knt., and Alice Brun, his wife. 1365.
57. Walter, 4th Baron Fitz-Walter. 1368.
58. Henry Percy, 1st Earl of Northumberland. 1390.
59. John "of Gaunt," see above No. 54. 4th seal. 1392.
60. Edmund Plantagenet, Duke of York, 5th son of Edward III. 1391.
61. Ingelram de Coucy, Earl of Bedford. 1366.
62. William de Beauchamp, 1st Baron Abergavenny. 1396.
63. Michael de la Pole, 3rd Earl of Suffolk. 1408.
64. Sir Maurice de Berkeley, Lord of Beverstone. 1428.
65. Thomas Plantagenet, Duke of Clarence, second son of Henry IV. 1413.
66. Humphrey Plantagenet, Duke of Gloucester, fourth son of Henry IV. 1426.
67. Sir James Ormond, Knt., Captain of Gournay, France. 1441.
68. John Darcy, Lord of Knayth, co. Lincoln. 1349.
69. Jasper Tudor, Earl of Pembroke. 1459.
70. John de la Pole, Earl of Lincoln. [1467–1487.]
71. John de Vere, 13th Earl of Oxford, Lord Great Chamberlain and Lord High Admiral. 1496.
72. Richard Grey, Earl of Kent, Baron Grey of Ruthyn. [1504–1523.]
73. Sir Robert Dudley, K.G., Earl of Leicester. 1566.
74. The same—another seal. [1563–1588.]

75. Charles Howard, 1st Earl of Nottingham, Lord High Admiral. 1601.

SEALS OF LADIES OF RANK.

76. Mary, daughter of Lawrence of Rouen. [Early 13th cent.]
77. Ydonia de Herste, Lady of Prumhelle, co. Kent. [13th cent.]
78. Mable de Gatton. [13th cent.]
79. Joan de Stuteville. [About 1224.]
80. Ela, Countess of Salisbury. [1226–1240.]
81. Margaret de Quincy, Countess of Winchester. [1219–1235.]
82. Margaret de Lacy, Countess of Lincoln and Pembroke. [1232–1240.]
83. Maud, daughter of William Luvetot, widow of Gerard, Baron Furnival. [About 1260.]
84. Alice de Lacy, Countess of Lincoln, daughter of the Marquis of Saluces. [About 1270.]
85. 86. Sir Hugh de Coleworthe, Knt., and Elizabeth his wife. [Late 13th cent.]
87. Isabel de Beaumont, widow of Sir John de Vescy. [1289–1311.]
88. Agnes de Percy, of co. Lincoln. [About 1200.]
89. Alice de Lacy, Countess of Lincoln, daughter and heiress of Henry the 3rd Earl. 1310.
90. Margaret de Neville. 1315.
91. Elizabeth de Burgh, Lady of Clare. 1335.
92. Elizabeth de Multon, wife of Walter de Bermyngham. 1341.
93. Matilda of Lancaster, Countess of Ulster. 1347.
94. Euphemia de Lacy, widow of Sir Walter de Heselarton, Knt. 1369.
95. Anne, Countess of Stafford, daughter of Thomas, Duke of Gloucester, youngest son of Edward III. 1434.
96. Margaret, Countess of Shrewsbury, daughter of Richard, Earl of Warwick. 1456.
97. Margaret, Countess of Salisbury, daughter of George, Duke of Clarence. 1514.

ILLUMINATIONS.

[Exhibited in cases, numbered 1–6, in the King's Library.]

Case 1.

1. Charter of Foundation of Newminster at Winchester, by King Edgar; A.D. 966. Written in gold; with a full-page miniature and elaborate border in gold and colours by an English artist. [*Cotton MS.* Vespasian A. viii.]
2. Psalter in *Latin*, with interlinear glosses in Anglo-Saxon. Miniatures, initials and borders, in colours, by English artists. Late 11th century. [*Arundel MS.* 60.]
3. The "Psychomachia" of Aurelius Prudentius, a *Latin* poem on the conflict between virtues and vices in the human soul, with glosses and notes in Anglo-Saxon. Outline drawings, tinted, by English artists. 11th century. [*Cotton MS.* Cleop. C. viii.]
4. The Gospels in *Latin*. The volume also contains a copy of a charter of King Cnut. Initials and borders in gold and colours, by English artists. 11th century. [*Royal MS.* 1 D. ix.]
5. Paraphrase in *Anglo-Saxon* of the Pentateuch and Book of Joshua, by Ælfric, Archbishop of Canterbury [d. 1006]. Outline and coloured drawings, by English artists. Early 11th century. [*Cotton MS.* Claudius B. iv.]
6. Psalter and Prayers, in *Latin*. Initials in gold and colours, by English artists. 13th century. [*Royal MS.* 2 A. xxii.]
7. Psalter, in *Latin*. Miniatures and initials, by English artists. Late 13th century. Belonged to John Grandison, Bishop of Exeter [1327–1369], who bequeathed it to Isabella, daughter of Edward III. [*Add. MS.* 21,926.]
8. Biblo, in *Latin*. Written and illuminated with initials and borders at Canterbury. 13th century. [*Burney MS.* 3.]
9. Bible, in *Latin*. Miniature-initials by French artists. Late 13th century. [27,694.]
10. Psalter, in *Latin*. Miniatures, initials and borders, by

Flemish artists. End of 13th century. [*Add. MS.* 30,029.]

11. Psalter, in *Latin*. Miniatures, initials and borders, by French artists. Late 13th century. [*Add. MS.* 17,868.]
12. Psalter, in *Latin*. Miniatures, initials and borders, by Flemish artists. Late 13th century. Belonged to Queen Mary I. [*Royal MS.* 2 B. iii.]
13. Psalter, in *Latin*. Miniatures, initials and borders, by Scandinavian artists. Belonged to Jacobus, son of Suno, brother and father of two bishops of Roeskilde in Denmark [d. 1246]. Early 13th century. [*Egerton MS.* 2652.]
14. Bible-History, in *Latin*. Outline drawings by French artists. End of 13th century. [*Add. MS.* 18,719.]
15. Psalter, in *Latin*. Miniatures, initials and borders, by French artists. Early 14th century. [*Add. MS.* 29,923.]
16. The Apocalypse in *Latin* and *French*. Miniatures by French artists. Early 14th century. Belonged to Vaudieu Abbey, near Liége. [*Add. MS.* 17,333.]
17. The Apocalypse, in *French*. Miniatures by English artists. Early 14th century. [*Royal MS.* 19 B. xv.]
18. The Apocalypse, in *Latin* and *French*. Miniatures by English artists. Early 14th century. [*Add. MS.* 18,633.]
19. Missal, in *Latin*. Miniatures, initials and borders, by French artists. 14th century. [*Harley MS.* 2891.]

Case 2.

20. Breviary, in *Latin*. Miniature-initials and borders, by Italian artists, closely following Byzantine models. Early 14th century. [*Add. MS.* 15,205.]
21. Lives of Saints, in *Italian*. Miniatures and initials, by Italian artists of the school of Giotto. 14th century. [*Add. MS.* 27,428.]
22. Ancient History, *in French*. Miniatures by artists of the South of France. Early 14th century. [*Add. MS.* 15,268.]
23. Ancient History, in *French*. Outline drawings, tinted, by artists of the South of France. Early 14th century. [*Royal MS.* 20 D. i.]
24. Bible, in *Latin*. Miniatures, initials and borders, by Italian artists. Early 14th century. [*Add. MS.* 18,720.]
25. Durandus "de divinis officiis." Miniatures, initials

and borders, by Italian artists. Early 14th century. [*Add. MS.* 31,032.]

26. Poems, in *Latin*, by Convenevole da Prato, the tutor of Petrarch, written for Robert of Anjou, King of Naples [1334–1342]. Miniatures by Italian artists. 14th century. [*Royal MS.* 6 E. ix.]
27. The "Divina Commedia" of Dante. Miniatures by Italian artists. 14th century. [*Egerton MS.* 943.]
28. Treatise on Virtues and Vices, in *Latin*, by a member of the family of Cocharelli of Genoa. Miniatures and coloured drawings of objects of natural history, executed probably by one of the family of Cibo, known as the Monk of Hyères. 14th century. [*Add. MS.* 28,841.]
29. Hours of the Virgin, in *Latin*. Miniatures, initials and borders, by Italian artists. 14th century. [*Add. MS.* 15,265.]

Case 3.

30. Epistle, in *French*, of Philippe de Mezières, for peace and friendship between Charles VI. of France and Richard II. of England, with a miniature containing a portrait of Richard II., and borders by French artists. End of 14th century. [*Royal MS.* 20 B. vi.]
31. Hours of the Virgin, in *Latin*. Miniatures, initials and borders, by French artists. Beginning of the 15th century. [*Add. MS.* 32,454.]
32. Bible History, in *French*. Miniatures, initials and borders, by French artists. 14th century. The MS. belonged to John II. of France, and was taken, with him, at the Battle of Poitiers, A.D. 1356. [*Royal MS.* 19 D. ii.]
33. "Histoire des Rois de France." Miniatures by French artists. Beginning of the 15th century. [*Royal MS.* 20 C. vii.]
34. Hours of the Virgin, in *Latin*. Miniatures, initials and borders, by Italian artists. Early 15th century. [*Add. MS.* 17,943.]
35. History of Alexander the Great, in *French*. Miniatures, initials and borders, by French artists. 15th century. [*Royal MS.* 20 B. xx.]
36. "Roman de la Rose." Miniatures, initials and borders in *camaïeu-gris*, by French artists. 15th century. [*Egerton MS.* 2022.]

37. Romances, in *French.* Miniatures, initials and borders, by French artists. 15th century. [*Cotton MS.* Nero D. ix.]
38. Hours of the Virgin and Psalter, in *Latin.* Miniatures, initials and borders, by English artists. Early 15th century. [*Royal MS.* 2 A. xviii.]
39. Hours of the Virgin and Psalter, in *Latin.* Miniatures, initials and borders, by English artists. 15th century. [*Harley MS.* 3000.]
40. Romances of chivalry, in *French.* Miniatures, initials and borders, in French style, by English artists. 15th century. The MS. was presented by John Talbot, Earl of Shrewsbury [d. 1453] to Margaret of Anjou, queen of Henry VI. [*Royal MS.* 15 E. vi.]
41. Hours of the Virgin, in *Latin.* Miniatures, initials and borders, by French artists. 15th century. [*Add. MS.* 18,751.]
42. Hours of the Virgin, in *Latin.* Miniatures, initials and borders, by French artists. 15th century. [*Add. MS.* 31,834.]
43. Hours of the Virgin, in *Latin.* Miniatures, initials and borders, by French artists. 15th century. [*Harley MS.* 2940.]
44. Froissart's Chronicle, in *French.* Miniatures, initials and borders, by French artists. Late 15th century. [*Harley MS.* 4380.]

Case 4.

45. Lectionary, in *Latin.* With a miniature representing the artist, named Sifer Was, offering the book to John, Lord Lovel, of Tichmersh [d. 1408]; and initials and borders. Beginning of the 15th century. [*Harley MS.* 7026.]
46. Bible-History, in *French.* Miniatures, initials and borders, by French artists. Executed for John, Duke of Berri, son of King John II. of France. Beginning of the 15th century. [*Harley MS.* 4382.]
47. Hours of the Virgin, in *Latin.* Miniatures, initials and borders, by French artists. 15th century. [*Harley MS.* 2971.]
48. Hours of the Virgin, in *Latin.* Miniatures, initials

and borders, by French artists. 15th century. [*Harley MS.* 2952.]

49. Hours of the Virgin, in *Latin.* Miniatures, initials and borders, by French artists. 15th century. [*Add. MS.* 18,192.]

50. Bible-History, to the death of Joshua, in *Italian.* Coloured drawings by Italian artists. Beginning of the 15th century. [*Add. MS.* 15,277.]

51. Hours of the Virgin, in *Latin.* Miniatures, initials and borders, by Italian artists. Late 15th century. [*Add. MS.* 19,417.]

52. Breviary in *Latin.* Initials and borders, by Italian artists. Late 15th century. Belonged to a member of the family of Medici. [*Add. MS.* 25,697.]

Case 5.

53. The Ethics of Aristotle, in *Spanish;* translated by Charles, Prince of Viana, for Alphonso V. of Aragon. Initials and borders, by Spanish artists. 15th century. [*Add. MS.* 21,120.]

54. Hours of the Virgin, in *Latin.* Initials and borders, by Spanish artists. Late 15th century. [*Add. MS.* 28,271.]

55. Hours of the Virgin, in *Latin.* Miniatures, initials and borders, by Spanish artists. Late 15th century. [*Add. MS.* 18,193.]

56. Plutarch's Lives of Great Men, in *Latin.* Miniatures, initials and borders, by Italian artists. 15th century. [*Add. MS.* 22,318.]

57. Hours of the Virgin, in *Dutch.* Miniatures, initials and borders, by Dutch artists. Late 15th century. [*Add. MS.* 15,267.]

58. Hours of the Virgin, in *Dutch.* Miniatures, initials and borders, by Dutch artists. Late 15th century. [*Add. MS.* 17,524.]

59. Breviary, in *Latin.* Miniatures, initials and borders, by Dutch artists. Late 15th century. [*Harley MS.* 2975.]

60. Breviary, in *Latin.* Initials and borders, by Italian artists. Late 15th century. [*Add. MS.* 15,260.]

Case 6.

61. Hours of the Virgin, in *Latin*. Miniatures, initials and borders, by Flemish artists. Late 15th century. [*Add. MS.* 15,677.]
62. Hours of the Virgin, in *Latin*. Miniatures, initials and borders, by Flemish artists. End of the 15th century. Belonged to a lady of the courts of Henry VII. and Henry VIII. [*Add. MS.* 17,012.]
63. Hours of the Virgin, in *Latin*. Miniatures, initials and borders, by Flemish artists. Beginning of the 16th century. Belonged to Henry VIII. [*King's MS.* 9.]
64. Hours of the Virgin, in *Latin*. Miniatures, initials and borders, by Flemish artists. Late 15th century. [*Add. MS.* 17,026.]
65. Hours of the Virgin, in *Latin*. Miniatures, initials and borders, by Flemish artists. End of the 15th century. [*Egerton MS.* 1149.]
66. "Splendor Solis": an alchemical work in *German*; A.D. 1582. Miniatures and borders in Flemish style, by German artists. [*Harley MS.* 3469.]
67. "Mystère de la Passion." Miniatures by French artists. Late 15th century. [*Royal MS.* 19 B. vi.]
68. Hours of the Virgin, in *Latin*. Miniatures, initials and borders, by French artists. Late 15th century. [*Add. MS.* 14,865.]
69. Hours of the Virgin, in *Latin*. Miniatures, initials and borders, by French artists. Late 15th century. [*Harley MS.* 2950.]
70. Hours of the Virgin, in *Latin*. Miniatures, initials and borders, by French artists. End of the 15th century. [*Harley MS.* 2863.]
71. Hours of the Virgin, in *Latin*. Miniatures, initials and borders, by French artists. Written and illuminated, A.D. 1525, for François de Dinteville, Bishop of Auxerre. [*Add. MS.* 18,854.]
72. "Le Trésor" or "Les sept articles de la Foi," by Jehan de Meung. Miniatures by French artists. Early 16th century. [*Egerton MS.* 940.]

At the further end of the King's Library is exhibited a selection of Bindings in six large upright cases; two of which contain Manuscripts, bound in various materials at different periods.

E. MAUNDE THOMPSON.

Dept. of MSS.,
February, 1887.

LONDON:
PRINTED BY WILLIAM CLOWES AND SONS, LIMITED,
STAMFORD STREET AND CHARING CROSS.

www.ingramcontent.com/pod-product-compliance
Lightning Source LLC
Chambersburg PA
CBHW031455270326
41930CB00007B/1020
9783337104986